# A Bike Trip
Across America

# A Bike Trip Across America

★ ★ ★ ★ ★ ★ ★

*A 3,411 Mile Journey of Discovery*

**Patrick McGinty**

Bywater Press
Bellingham, Washington

©2020 by Patrick T. McGinty. All rights reserved
Some names in the narrative have been changed or omit
surnames to protect privacy.

Published by Bywater Press, Bellingham, Washington.
www.bywaterpress.com

First edition, first printing.        C D E F G H I K
ISBN: 978-1-7330675-1-5 (print)
ISBN: 978-1-7330675-4-6 (ebook)

*This book is dedicated to my mom, Theresa McGinty, who has been a loving, supportive mother and who unknowingly inspired me with her honesty and caution.*

*(NOTE: I'd like to take this chance to belatedly apologize to Mom if any of my lifetime of "crazy" adventures has caused her any undue stress, sleepless nights, or premature aging.)*

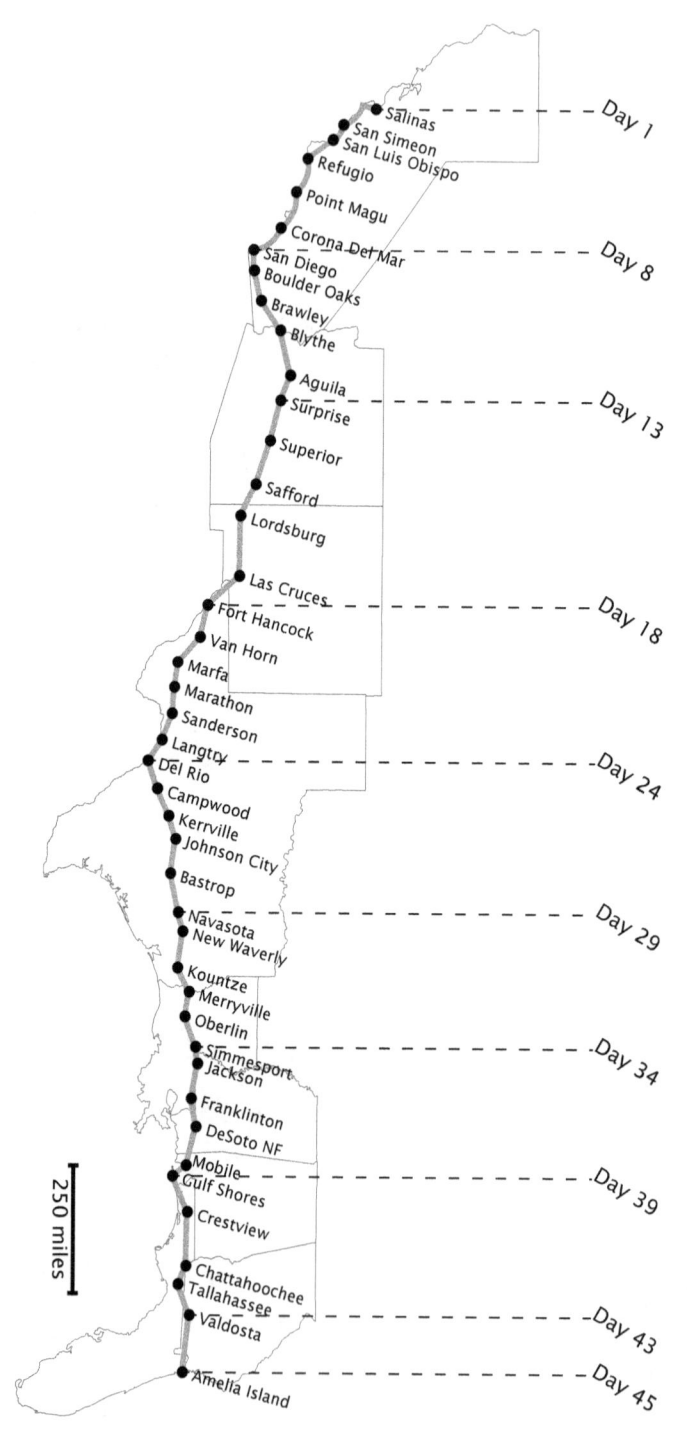

# Table of Contents

Overview Route Map . . . . . . . . . . . . . . . . . . . viii
Introduction . . . . . . . . . . . . . . . . . . . . . . . 1
Chapter 1: My Metamorphosis Into an Adventurous Spirit   3
Chapter 2: Why I Biked Across America . . . . . . . .    9
Chapter 3: Gear . . . . . . . . . . . . . . . . . . . . . 11
Chapter 4: Finishing the Pacific Coast Bicycle Route –
    Dreams, Big Sur, Beaches . . . . . . . . . . . . . 15
  Day 1 – (52 miles) Salinas, California Amtrak Station to
    Pfeifer Big Sur State Park . . . . . . . . . . . . 17
  Day 2 – (65 miles) Pfeifer Big Sur State Park to San
    Simeon State Park Campground . . . . . . . . . 22
  Day 3 – (40 miles) San Simeon State Park Campground
    to San Luis Obispo . . . . . . . . . . . . . . . . 27
  Day 4 – (90 miles) San Luis Obispo to Refugio State
    Beach Campground . . . . . . . . . . . . . . . . 29
  Day 5 – (80 miles) Refugio State Beach Campground to
    Sycamore Canyon Campground . . . . . . . . . 33
  Day 6 – (94 miles) Sycamore Canyon Campground to
    Corona Del Mar, California . . . . . . . . . . . . 36
  Day 7 – (96 miles) Corona Del Mar to San Diego . . . 40
Chapter 5: The Southern Tier Bicycle Route Begins –
    Challenge, Desert, People Power . . . . . . . . . 47
  Day 8 – (60 miles) San Diego to Boulder Oaks
    Campground . . . . . . . . . . . . . . . . . . . . 47
  Day 9 – (94 miles) Boulder Oaks Campground to
    Brawley, California . . . . . . . . . . . . . . . . 50
  Day 10 – (94 miles) Brawley to Blythe, California . . . 54
  Day 11 – (90 miles) Blythe, California to Aguila, Arizona 58
  Day 12/13 – (59 miles/zero-day) Aguila to Surprise,
    Arizona . . . . . . . . . . . . . . . . . . . . . . . 60
  Day 14 – (94 miles) Surprise to Superior, Arizona . . . 64
  Day 15 – (110 miles) Superior to Safford, Arizona . . . 66
  Day 16 – (76 miles) Safford, Arizona to Lordsburg, New
    Mexico . . . . . . . . . . . . . . . . . . . . . . . 71
  Day 17 – (120 miles) Lordsburg to Las Cruces, New
    Mexico . . . . . . . . . . . . . . . . . . . . . . . 73

Day 18 – (103 miles) Las Cruces, New Mexico to Fort
    Hancock, Texas . . . . . . . . . . . . . . . 76
Chapter 6: West Texas – Remote, Surprises, Hill Country . 81
    Day 19 – (70 miles) Fort Hancock to Van Horn, Texas . 81
    Day 20 – (74 miles) Van Horn to Marfa, Texas . . . . 83
    Day 21 – (60 miles) Marfa to Marathon, Texas . . . . 85
    Day 22 – (54 miles) Marathon to Sanderson, Texas . . 87
    Day 23 – (60 miles) Sanderson to Langtry, Texas . . . 88
    Day 24 – (58 miles) Langtry to Del Rio, Texas . . . . . 90
    Day 25 – (78 miles) Del Rio to outside Campwood,
       Texas . . . . . . . . . . . . . . . . . . . . 94
    Day 26 – (87 miles) Outside Campwood to Kerrville,
       Texas . . . . . . . . . . . . . . . . . . . . 95
    Day 27 – (83 miles) Kerrville to Johnson City, Texas . . 98
    Day 28 – (88 miles) Johnson City to Bastrop, Texas . . 103
Chapter 7: East Texas – Dogs, Thunderstorms, Tornados . 107
    Day 29 – (108 miles) Bastrop to Navasota, Texas . . . 107
    Day 30 – (42 miles) Navasota to New Waverly (stayed
       in Conroy, Texas) . . . . . . . . . . . . . . 110
    Day 31 – (84 miles) New Waverly to Kountze, Texas . 112
    Day 32 – (63 miles) Kountze, Texas to Merryville,
       Louisiana . . . . . . . . . . . . . . . . . . 114
Chapter 8: The South (Louisiana, Mississippi, Alabama) –
    More Dogs, Warmshowers, Lovely People . . . . 121
    Day 33 – (56 miles) Merryville to Oberlin, Louisiana . . 121
    Day 34 – (106 miles) Oberlin to Simmesport, Louisiana 124
    Day 35 – (51 miles) Simmesport to Jackson, Louisiana . 126
    Day 36 – (78 miles) Jackson to Franklinton, Louisiana . 128
    Day 37 – (96 miles) Franklinton, Louisiana to DeSoto
       National Forest, Mississippi . . . . . . . . . . 130
    Day 38 – (63 miles) Desoto National Forest, Mississippi
       to Mobile, Alabama . . . . . . . . . . . . . 131
    Day 39 – (66 miles) Mobile to Gulf Shores, Alabama . 132
Chapter 9: The Southern Tier Bicycle Route Ride Ends
    (Florida, Georgia, Florida) – Food, Gratitude,
    Accomplishment . . . . . . . . . . . . . . . 135
    Day 40 – (98 miles) Gulf Shores, Alabama to Crestview,
       Florida . . . . . . . . . . . . . . . . . . . 135
    Day 41 – (110 miles) Crestview to Chattahoochee,
       Florida . . . . . . . . . . . . . . . . . . . 137

Day 42 – (44 miles) Chattahoochee to Tallahassee,
    Florida . . . . . . . . . . . . . . . . . . 139
Day 43 – (85 miles) Tallahassee, Florida to Valdosta,
    Georgia . . . . . . . . . . . . . . . . . . 140
Day 44 – Zero-Day, Valdosta, Georgia . . . . . . . . 143
Day 45 – (132 miles) Valdosta, Georgia to Amelia
    Island, Florida . . . . . . . . . . . . . . . 144
Chapter 10: Bike Trip Stats . . . . . . . . . . . . . 151
Chapter 11: Cost Breakdown of Bike Trip . . . . . . . . 153
Chapter 12: Lessons Learned . . . . . . . . . . . . 155
Chapter 13: Last Reflections . . . . . . . . . . . . 161
Epilogue . . . . . . . . . . . . . . . . . . . . . 163
Author Bio . . . . . . . . . . . . . . . . . . . . 165

# Introduction

During my twenties, perhaps while having a quarter-life crisis, the biggest question I used to ask was, "If I had only six months to live, what would I do?" The answer was never working more, but it was more likely to be *go on an adventure*. To travel to a far-off destination that I always dreamed of experiencing, to learn about other cultures, landscapes, and myself. It was a bonus if the place was sunny, warm, and had lots of beautiful women. Once I made a decision, I would make it happen. I'd earn enough money to fly to Hawaii, then Alaska, then around the world, living frugally out of a backpack. Life was good. Life was fun. The adventures added up, and I was thrilled with the places, people, and exploits I experienced. But then, life happened. I had to start a career, get a mortgage, get a serious girlfriend, and start thinking about retirement plans. Yikes!! It was all good until the inevitable mid-life crisis and the questioning of what is life all about? Is it about working until I retire at 65, but am too feeble to go on big, epic adventures? Is it about giving my life energy to an employer for the opportunity to buy a bigger house, the sportiest car, or the newest cell phone? Is it about making lots of money, to buy things, in order to impress people I don't know or like? I long ago didn't want to participate in the rat race, and I didn't see the reason to be "keeping up with the Joneses."

In the spring of 2017, I was 52 years old, bored, and uninspired in my job. Luckily, I was a lifelong saver and minimalist, and because of this I had a decent financial cushion to have options. I realized my greatest need at the time was a challenge that got me excited to get out of bed in the morning. What to do? My answer: to take control, throw caution to the wind, and go on adventures I'd been dreaming about over the last few years. So that is what I did. I read somewhere that a mid-life crisis for a man composed of buying a red sports car and getting a young girlfriend to relive their reckless adolescent youth; however, my mid-life crisis was different: I bought a bike and a backpack. I didn't want to get to the end of my life and wonder "what if?" or have any regrets. I didn't want to be some Walter Mitty type who dreamed dreams and didn't have the courage to pursue them. I wanted to stomp on my inner Walter Mitty and make my dreams of epic adventures a reality.

## INTRODUCTION

My final day of work was June 7, 2017, and my Independence Day was June 8 as I jumped on my bike and biked down the Pacific Coast from Longview, Washington to Monterey, California. I thoroughly enjoyed the experience and wanted more. Over the next year and a half, I would hike the John Muir Trail, hike all over the North Cascades, and the Rockies in both Canada and the US. Life was now on my terms, and adventure was at the forefront. However, one trip I always wanted to do but had serious hesitation over was biking across America. It wouldn't be until the spring of 2019 that I would take on the challenge and be rewarded for it.

In the pages that follow, I will share how my adventurist spirit slowly manifested during my youth, how it blossomed from a seemingly innocent question to my mom and her epic, motivational response. I will share with you my "Why?" of biking across America and my day-to-day adventures that will include what I was thinking, eating, where I was sleeping, people I was meeting, what challenges I had to overcome, what it felt like to reach the Atlantic Ocean, and other surprising things that happened over 45 days.

Biking across America by myself was a huge undertaking. I had my fears and trepidations in the beginning, but I overcame them by just jumping on my bike and moving forward every day. I learned a great deal about myself, my country, and the power of people. It was an opportunity to stretch my comfort zone and realize that achieving small goals leads to accomplishing significant goals. What follows is a journey of discovery through a great country filled with wonderful, delightful characters, epic landscapes, and unforgettable memories.

# Chapter 1: My Metamorphosis Into an Adventurous Spirit

*"Life is a daring adventure or nothing at all."*
– Helen Keller

Who hasn't wanted to get away from the "normal" daily grind of the working life and, instead, challenge yourself to accomplish a big, bold, audacious goal? A goal that stretches your comfort zone enough to scare the shit out of you but at the same time seems possible. A goal you always dreamed about but didn't have the time, money, or gumption to take it on. That is where I was in the spring of 2019. In transition, not wanting to do the "normal" thing but to challenge myself in a daring manner that would pump some adrenalin in me and resurrect my inner explorer.

The idea of biking across America came from my idiosyncratic interest in looking at maps during my free time and coming up with new ways to explore the United States. Having driven across the country many times, I thought, why not bike across it? But it seemed so far, and it would take so long. It seemed impossible; however, I had seen and heard of many other regular people who accomplished it and had grown from the experience. It was undoubtedly adventurous; however, as with most of my big, bold trips I've contemplated in the past, I always had hesitation in committing to daring adventures. I believe my delay was because I did not grow up in a family that were risk-takers or valued exploratory undertakings.

I believe we all have an adventurous spirit inside us that is just dying to manifest itself in our daily lives. Whether this adventurous spirit shows itself in our careers, relationships, outdoor adventures, or other human realms, it is ever-present in us waiting to reveal itself by taking risks, exploring undiscovered horizons, and challenging our comfort zone. However, for many of us, our adventurous spirit is thwarted by our to-do lists, obligations, social norms, political realities, and pursuit of success. For most, taking risks is scary, perhaps dangerous, and not what most people do, so we play it safe and admire others for their adventurous spirit.

However, even at a young age, I had a desire within me to be (as Teddy Roosevelt put it) "the man in the arena" daring greatly. To go out into the big, bad world and discover what was and what was not possible. To adventure to far off lands and to go where others, including my parents, would dare not to go.

When I was 13, my adventurous spirit was sprouting as I began to love riding my brown sporty three-speed bicycle 25 miles round trip from my home in Arlington, Massachusetts to Revere Beach and back through dangerous traffic, no bike lanes, no helmet, and no approval from my parents. To this day, I think the idea was crazy as I was still small enough to be barely seen over the hood of a car, but to me, it was a fun adventure. I wanted to let my parents know, but they would disapprove and be worried, so I would say I was going out for a bike ride. Adventure to my parents was somewhat limited. It might entail something like driving to grandma's house or the hardware store and back. Even at a young age, I realized there were horizons to explore and fears to be conquered.

My biking adventures would continue as I got older as I would begin heading west to a place called Walden Pond in Concord. It was a 35-mile round trip ride that would take most of a day biking up and down Massachusetts Avenue, where I thought nothing of biking with cars a foot away from my bike. When I arrived at Walden Pond, I would walk around the pond to the quiet section where I later learned Henry David Thoreau had his cabin. Initially, I did not know who Henry David Thoreau was or what he represented; however, there was something peaceful about the place, and I felt at home. Later, when I found out who he was after reading his book *Walden*, I realized his words and philosophy spoke to my soul, and the seeds of simplicity, minimalism, and self-reliance were planted. These seeds would become part of my living philosophy that guides me to this day.

While my adventurous spirit would reveal itself periodically in my late teens and early twenties, my parents never approved of it. Most of my friends didn't understand me, so I relegated myself to doing what was considered "normal." I concentrated on getting an education, being a good worker, and fitting into a healthy working lifestyle. However, something in the back of my mind said I wanted something more, something different. I knew of other friends, usually more well off than my family, who were traveling to Europe and throughout the US having great adventures. I always admired their adventurous spirit, and I wondered why I couldn't travel like them. I thought it was because I had no money. I later realized I had a self-limiting belief that was fostered by my lack of confidence in myself and my lack of parental support. Up to my early twenties, my parents' support with my plans was still important to me. However, I never wanted to be like my parents. They were caught in a working life cycle where accumulating beautiful things, watching lots of television, and slaving at jobs for a paycheck to pay for it was their life. I think Bruce Springsteen said it best in the chorus to his song "Factory," where he sings in an exhausting, slow, and desperate chorus "it's the work, the working, just the working life." While I knew to work was vital as it paid the bills, I also felt there must be a more exciting way to live.

Life's crucial moments seem to happen from seemingly mundane events. My adventurous spirit was growing stronger in my early twenties as I attended college at North Adams State College in North Adams, Massachusetts. It was probably no coincidence that the college was the furthest state college from my parents in the state of Massachusetts. A critical moment in my life would occur after taking an eye-opening class called "The History of Ideas." In the course, I became fascinated with contemporary Soviet history that included learning about Mikhail Gorbachev, *perestroika*, and *glasnost*. After taking the class, I saw an advertisement that a history professor at my college was organizing a Winter Study trip to the Soviet Union for 23 days. The trip cost was $1,100, all expenses included. It may surprise most people, but I was paying my college bills at the time with cash I had earned delivering newspapers. I would go to the Bursar's office and pay my tuition and fees with the twenties, tens, fives, and one-dollar bills I had earned from my paper route. At the time, I was probably one of the highest-paid newspaper deliverers in Massachusetts as I made as much as $700 a week delivering Boston Globes, Boston Heralds, and the New York Times. I made a lot of money in the mid-1980's doing what most people didn't want to do because you had to wake up early and be done by 7 am. I was a hustler and would bust ass to make as much as I could. If someone was sick or a route needed delivering, I always volunteered to do it. I loved the peace, quiet, and freedom of the early mornings. I was making much more money than the office managers and most of my friends who had real jobs where they had to wear a suit to work. I even once made over $2,000 in just Christmas tips from my newspaper customers. So, paying my tuition and also being able to afford to pay for the Soviet Union trip was no problem.

Once I decided I wanted to go on the Soviet Union trip, I still was hesitant because of the cost (to me a lot of money to spend on a trip). Before I committed to going, I wanted to pass the idea by my parents to see what they thought of the plan to go to the Soviet Union. To this point in my life, I had never been out of North American and had only spent a drunken weekend in Montreal and walked briefly into Tijuana, Mexico. Little did I know a life-changing event was about to unfold that would be a catalyst to a seismic change in my life. The seismic shift would enrich my life beyond anything I could comprehend at the time.

The seismic event started innocently as a touch base phone call to my mom to let her know how college was going. After giving her an update that never included wild parties attended or how much wiffleball I was playing compared to actual class time. I could tell she was approving of my update and that I was happy and learning lots in college. But then the question that would change it all. I asked, "Mom, I am thinking of going on a winter study trip to the Soviet Union with a college professor and a group of students; what do you think?" I asked her this question in a relaxed manner. I was excited about the opportunity and recognized with all the change going on in the Soviet Union that it was an opportunity to see history unfold with my own eyes. Initially, there was an eerie silence from my mom. The silence was so long I thought I might have offended her, but then my mom responded with an emphatic "WHAT, ARE YOU CRAZY?" Her response blew me away. I was shocked by its power and delivery. Before I could comprehend her message, she started spouting off how dangerous it was and something about the red menace that would have made Joseph McCarthy blush. I felt like I was listening to the cold war rhetoric of the past forty years. I slowly digested the fact that my mom didn't think it was a good idea. However, a life-changing thought was beginning to come over me that would change the course of my life.

It dawned on me that if I wanted to be different than my parents and not lead a "normal life," then I had to do things that they thought were "crazy." By doing "crazy" things, I would burst out of my parent's expectation bubble and become the person I wanted to become. My conversation with my mom turned out to be a tremendous revelation to me. I didn't want to offend my mom or my dad, but I had to live my own life the way I wanted to, so I needed to make bold decisions that were best for me and my future. I thanked my mom for her opinion of my trip idea. I announced to her that I was planning on going and paying for it with my funds. She still thought I was out of my mind but knew she could not stop me.

I did participate in winter study in the Soviet Union. It was an eye-opening experience that was life-changing in many ways and proved to be a catalyst to other adventures in life. After returning from the Soviet Union, whenever I wasn't sure about a new experience that stretched my comfort zone, I would call my mom to get her opinion. She would freely state, "What, are you crazy?", or a variant of that statement which meant to me, "DO IT." For example, Mom, I'm going to Alaska, what do you think? –"What, are you out of your mind?" – YES!!! Mom, I am thinking of flying around the world, what do you think? – "What, are you a nut?" – YES!! Mom, I am thinking of teaching English in Japan, what do you think? – "Why don't you get a real job!?!" – YES!! And on and on and on throughout my twenties, thirties, and beyond. Perhaps, it was my mom's worst nightmare. Her strong reaction to my bold ideas helped shape who I am, what I experienced in life, and how I see the world.

Even at the age of 53, I would go back to my reliable well of motivation, my 81-year young mom, and ask her what she thought of me biking across America? Her response, "WHAT, ARE YOU CRAZY?" It never gets old. Even with my mom's advancing age, my mom still knows how to help me stretch my comfort zone and just do it. Thanks, Mom!!

## Chapter 2: Why I Biked Across America

*"If you're not willing to risk the unusual, you will have to settle for the ordinary."*
– Jim Rohn

"Why on earth do I want to bike across the United States?" A question, not just asked by my mom, but many friends and acquaintances. While it was a crazy idea to many and perhaps a tremendous waste of time and resources to others, it was also bold. It would appeal to many people's adventurous spirit, whether fully developed or not. People who knew me intimately were not surprised. I had just recently biked a portion of the Pacific Coast Bicycle Route, hiked the John Muir Trail, and had quite the extensive travel adventure resume. It made such as undertaking just the next step in challenging myself.

My "Why?" came down to the following: the challenge, the opportunity to experience the southern culture, and the timing.

**1 - The challenge:** Just looking at a map of America renders the thought of biking across it look unfathomable. It is funny because I initially contemplated biking across America during the fall of 2018. I had a vision of surprising a friend by stopping by his office in Georgia. Then heading up to visit family in the Boston area while attending my 35th high school reunion. My arrival by bike would be quite shocking to my former classmates: Just think about how fit I would have been at the gathering. However, after driving back from a road trip from Colorado to my home base of Bellingham, Washington, in September of 2018, I was bored. I couldn't fathom the thought of actually biking the fifteen hundred miles, or the idea of biking across America, which would be at least three thousand miles. The fact it seemed impossible was the reason to go for it. Now was the time because I had the time, money, and ability to take the challenge. Even though the idea of biking across America scared the shit out of me.

**2 - To experience the southern US:** I have traveled to all fifty states, including four times to Hawaii, and I lived in Alaska for almost five years. I have also traveled to twenty-seven countries. However, I had never spent a lot of time in the southern states and wanted to experience the southwest culture and cuisine, real tacos in Texas, and southern charm. By cycling through the south, I would expand my horizons by biking in a desert, in the remoteness of West Texas, and through cool cities such as San Diego, Phoenix, and Austin, Texas.

**3 - The timing:** In March of 2019, I was in transition between jobs. I was taking the time to complete various adventures I always wanted to do while I still had cartilage in my knees. Most of my hiking trips were made during the summer months when the snows melted in the higher elevations. According to the Adventure Cycling Association (ACA), there were three main routes that crossed the United States – the Northern Tier, the TransAmerica Bicycle Trail (which goes through the middle of the US), and the Southern Tier. I could complete the southern tier in spring, as opposed to the Northern Tier and Transcontinental Bicycle Route, which would be cold and snowy in the spring months. I would start in March and end in May. Starting at the end of March was the ideal time to avoid the heat, storms, and tornado season. It would prove to be a perfect time.

## Chapter 3: Gear

*"There is no bad weather, only bad gear."*
*– quote from REI ad*

Your gear can make or break your trip. It can also affect your comfort and chances of completing your journey. Just about all of the equipment I used on my trip across America was adventure gear I had already purchased for past hiking and biking trips. The only new items I would buy were an inflatable pillow and a Schwalbe Marathon Plus tire for my back wheel. Below, is a list of gear I used on my trip:

**Bike:** 2016 REI Novara Randonée steel frame touring bike with a bike rack. I replaced the seat with a more comfortable seat from another bike I owned and put on Shimano clip-on pedals. I also replaced one of the Schwalbe Marathon tires (I brought it along as a spare) with a Schwalbe Marathon Plus in the rear for added puncture protection. I had two water bottle holders with two water bottles. A front and rear fender. And a puncture kit bag under my seat that held a spare tire tube, a CO2 gun and cartridge, pliers, and three tire levers. I also wore a short-sleeved bike shirt, padded bike shorts, helmet, bike shoes with clip-on, half-fingered bike gloves, Pearl Izumi (white) sun sleeves, and sunglasses at all times.

I used a four-bag system with no front panniers (only two large, waterproof Ortlieb bags for my rear panniers):

**Front Ortlieb Handlebar Bag (waterproof):** It held my big three – (1) cell phone, (2) prescription glasses, and (3) my wallet. It also contained a large Anker recharger, change, and a multitool. A tube of SPF 50 sunscreen, a headlamp, a portable rear light (used at night and in tunnels), snacks, and a can of HALT dog pepper spray. On my cell phone, I purchased and downloaded an electronic version of the Adventure Cycling Association Pacific Coast Bicycle Route maps and the Southern Tier Bicycle Route maps. I found the maps very helpful and easy to use.

**Right Yellow Ortlieb Pannier:** This pannier held my 20 degree down sleeping bag (wrapped in a garbage bag for added rain protection), an inflatable Thermarest pad, a Sea to Summit inflatable pillow, and my rain gear – one waterproof yellow jacket, one pair of waterproof pants, a pair of waterproof booties, and a yellow waterproof rain cover for

# GEAR

my helmet. I left a large pedal wrench at the bottom of my bag. I also attached my black flexible Kryptonite bike lock to this bag for quick access.

**Extra-Large Blue Water-Proof Dry Bag:** My dry bag was attached to the rear rack between the two loaded panniers. The waterproof bag held the two-person MSR Hubba-Hubba tent, my Teva's, and three extra 1.5-liter water bottles when in the desert. One spare Schwalbe Marathon tire under the bag. The bag and spare tire were held onto the rack by three medium bungee cords.

**Left Yellow Ortlieb Pannier:** This pannier carried my clothes, cooking gear, food, and miscellaneous items. My clothes were kept in a garbage bag as added protection to stay dry. The pannier included 2 full-length bike tights (one for sleeping when cold), 1 spare pair of bike shorts, 2 long sleeve shirts (one for sleeping in), 1 black long sleeve fleece, 1 short-sleeve bike top, 1 pair of light running shorts,

1 warm hat and 1 pair of full-fingered bike gloves, 3 pair of short bike socks, 1 bamboo underwear (to sleep in), and 1 neck buff (that I hardly wore). My cooking set-up included a small pocket-rocket stove, a large stainless-steel pot with a fork, spoon, lighter, sponge, chlorine tablets, and camping towel in the pot. Once I got off the train, I bought a large gas canister for the stove at REI in Marina. Among the miscellaneous items were a large tube of Chamois Butt'r Cream, one bottle of White Lightening chain lube, another spare tire tube, a bike pump, and a hygiene bag with toothpaste, toothbrush, soap, razor, and a small roll of duct tape.

At most, my gear, when I weighed it in Phoenix, with the full complement of 6 liters of water (for the desert) and loaded with food, was 58 lbs. My bike weighed about 32 lbs. It took a little getting used to riding with the extra weight. I found it stable and had no problems when I picked up speed going downhill and around corners. Going up a steep hill could be more challenging, but an excellent touring bike has a wide range of low gears to help you with the challenge. It is also essential to have a steel-framed bike because all the weight adds a lot of stress to your bike frame.

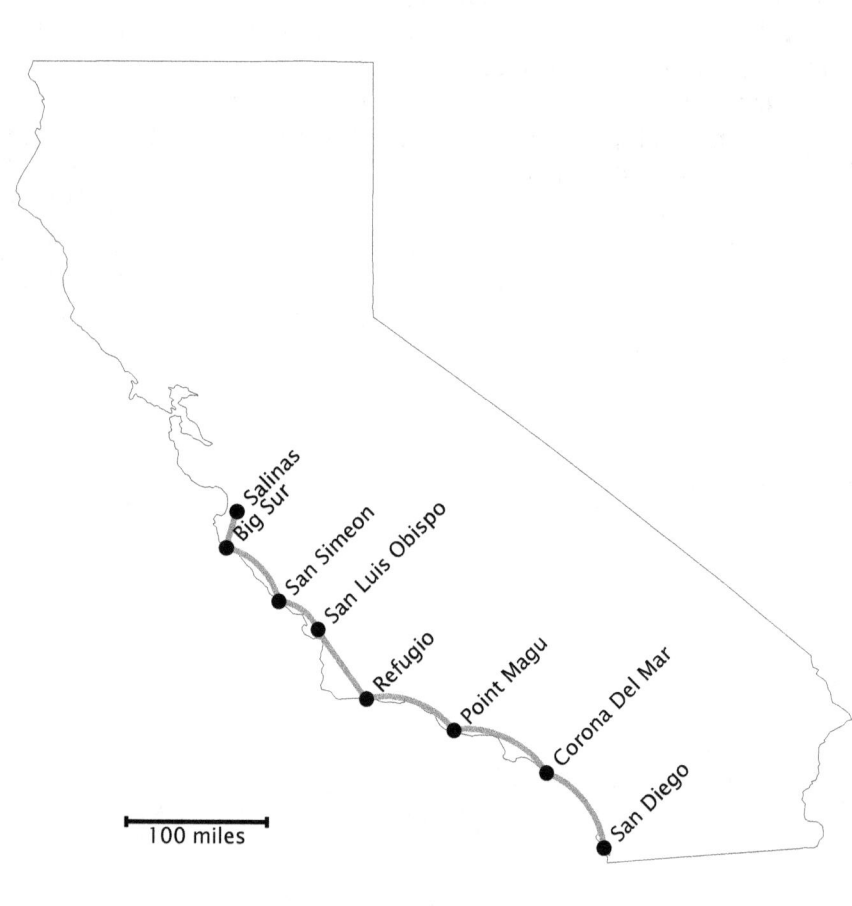

## Chapter 4: Finishing the Pacific Coast Bicycle Route – Dreams, Big Sur, Beaches

*"Stop being afraid of what could go wrong and start being excited about what could go right."*
– Tony Robbins

After months thinking about biking across the USA, it was time to take on the challenge. My alarm clock rang at 5 am on a Saturday, and I was excited to get started. I tried to maintain my usual daily routine by taking a shower, eating oatmeal, and making myself a pot of coffee. I had already packed my bike the night before so that I would be less likely to forget anything.

While I would be heading out on Saturday morning March 25th, I knew my bike ride would not start until about 1 pm on Monday, March 27th. My Amtrak ticket was for a Sunday morning departure out of Seattle, and my travel time was 26 hours to Salinas, California, with arrival at 12:30 pm on Monday. Since I got the ticket over two months in advance, my ticket only cost $96 plus an extra $20 to place my bike on the train without putting in a bike box. Not breaking my bike down was essential to me because I am not mechanically inclined, and breaking down and reassembling my bike again would have been burdensome.

It was weird to leave my condo to start the trip because I knew that once I left, I was committed and would not be back to my place of residence unless I completed the tour or I died. It seems a rather morbid thought, but I noticed I had a lot of various fears running through my imagination over the last week of preparation. I had premonitions such as, What if I got hit or run over by a truck? Or stabbed by a gang member in Los Angeles? Or abducted by the Russian mafia?

It seems so irrational now and is probably a symptom of watching too much television in my youth and too many recent new shows. It ran through my mind that this could be the last time I am in my condo that I have lived in for thirteen years. It is funny that I would think such weird thoughts as death being even a possibility. I had been on many adventures all over the world and recently hiked the John Muir Trail and biked down the West Coast of the US from Longview, Washington to Monterey in 2017 and never did the thought of death ever enter my mind; however with the recent death of my dad less than six months ago and talking to my mom about updating her will and directives got me thinking about the fragility of my own life. Before I left for my tour, I even completed my will and directives as well as took out added medical and evacuation insurance. My actions were a sign of how far over my comfort zone I thought this trip was and that anything was possible when you are out in remote, unfamiliar places, including death.

Even with my pains of sentimentality about leaving my condo and thoughts of possible death, I knew what I needed to do. I needed to get on my bike and start riding to Bellingham center so I could catch my bus on time. Before I left, being the minimalist and frugal guy that I am, I shut off all my breakers in my electrical box, and I shut off my water so that there could be no electrical fires to unnecessarily worry about or the possibility of slow leaks or floods that could become a substantial financial burden. It was important to me that my place was secure and that nothing could distract me while I was taking on a significant challenge in biking across the USA. Also, the shutting of the electrical fuse box would save me on my electric bill, and every little saving would be beneficial to me, considering I was about to spend over $3,000 to achieve a dream.

I took two uneventful bus rides to Everett, Washington, where my friend Mark Polin was letting me stay in his condo for the night. I was now closer to the real start of the adventure by being one short ride to the Seattle Amtrak Station. I was very much appreciative of having Mark willing to put me up for a night and then wake up early to drop me off in Seattle.

Mark dropped me off early at the Amtrak Station, and it gave me time to contemplate the challenging bike trip. As I ruminated, some of the fears started resurfacing, and I even had a brief thought of calling it off, but once the conductor loaded my bike onto the train, I was 100% committed to completing the challenge of biking to the Atlantic Ocean.

Something is soothing about train travel as you can relax and find things to distract you like a book, music, videos, a movie, or planning out your future. I was lucky the train was not crowded, and I got two seats for the price of one. I did try to sleep some, but it was not the most comfortable trying to sleep upright with my head against the window. It was also not conducive to a good night's sleep for the train to make multiple stops while you are trying to get REM sleep.

The train journey seemed to go by quick, and when we were less than one hour from the Salinas stop, I decided to review my gear. My gear was in good order except for one of my bike shoes. I noticed that the front of my right shoe was starting to separate at the toe. It looked like the kind of situation that could get worse. I decided to wrap some duct tape around the toe and in the middle of my bike shoe. It looked slightly tacky with the silver stripes on my shoe, but I felt it was practical in that my shoe might last a little while longer before I needed to buy new bike shoes. I was hoping they would last at least until San Diego but also hoped I never needed to purchase new bike shoes because I wanted to save the money. It also wouldn't be wrong if the shoes lasted to Florida, and I threw them out once the ride was over, so then I would not have to carry or mail them home.

## Day 1 – (52 miles) Salinas, California Amtrak Station to Pfeifer Big Sur State Park

*"The journey of a thousand miles begins with one step."*
– Lao Tze

The moment I was finally waiting for had arrived. The train pulled into the Salinas Amtrak Station, and it was time to start the journey. I gathered my bags and trotted quickly to the far baggage car that seemed like a mile away as there were quite a few cars between me and the baggage car. I thought that by the time I arrived at the baggage car, my bike would be out on the platform, or at least the baggage handler would be in the process of delivering my bike to the platform. However, that was not the case. There was no movement in the baggage car. I started growing concerned that something was wrong. I was very geared up to get started, but I needed my bike to do it. I dropped all my bags on the platform and started to find an Amtrak official to find out why my bike was not on the platform. I could see that the train officials were quickly getting everyone on the train and were ready to leave. I became a bit frantic in finding an Amtrak official. I found one just as they were saying "all aboard." The friendly Amtrak official could not give me the right answer to why my bike was not on the platform, so she banged on the baggage claim car to get the handler's attention.

Once we saw the baggage handler through the window of the baggage car, it looked like she was relaxing and eating lunch without any concern about unloading a bike. The baggage handler opened the cargo door, and at the same time, the Amtrak official and I asked about a green bicycle for the Salinas station. The baggage handler seemed clueless, which didn't make me feel confident. I started having evil thoughts about someone having stolen it, or the bike was dropped off to the wrong station; however, the baggage handler brought out a bike that was mine. Somehow during transit, the ticket on the bike that showed the bike's destination had been ripped off. It was lucky I did some assertive asking because the train was getting ready to move on without dropping off my bike. I thanked the Amtrak official. My bike trip could now officially start.

Before I started, I wanted to make sure I filled my water bottles and that I used the bathroom. Once I took care of my needs and packed my bike, I left the train station full of energy and headed for REI in Marina, where I needed to buy some camping gas for my stove. As I was riding, I had many thoughts in my head, but mostly I was thinking of making sure I was going the right direction and that I take the next left-hand turn onto the correct road. The traffic was a little heavy, but I was sure the traffic would be much more hectic as I got closer to Los Angeles. The first few miles were flat, and within the hour, I had made it to REI.

I get asked what I think about when I am riding, and the answer has mostly to do with logistics. While at REI, I contemplated buying a handlebar holder for my Android but decided against it because I didn't like how secure my phone would be in the holder, and I thought there were better options than the ones REI had at the time. If need be, I just placed my cell phone in my handlebar bag, which proved to be cumbersome, but it was the best I could do at the time. As the trip progressed, the cell phone holder would be one of the items I wish I invested in at the beginning of the journey.

Once I left REI, my next goal was to get myself onto the Fort Ord Dunes State Park bike trail along the dunes overlooking Monterey Bay. Whenever I see the ocean beyond the dunes, I marvel at the beauty; however, it also reminds me that only a few years ago, John Denver died just north of here in a plane crash at the young age of 53, my current age. It pains me that such a beautiful soul was killed in such a beautiful place. Once I got myself to the Fort Ord Dunes State Park bike trail that headed to Monterey, I would then concentrate on getting to the McDonalds in Monterey for a quick bite. My original plan was to have an easy first day by camping in Monterey; however, since the weather was clear, and not rainy as predicted, I decided I would challenge myself the first day and accomplish another dream of camping among the redwoods in Pfeifer Big Sur State Park. The park had a hiker/biker campsite, so they would only charge $6 to camp. The only problem was I had to bike the 52 miles up some good-sized hills in less than 5 hours.

After a quick meal at McDonalds, which would certainly not be my last, I headed up the good-sized hill to Carmel. I made it to Highway 1, which was very busy with cars. There was a decent bike lane, and the traffic flowed smoothly. Before I hit the hills of Big Sur, I had to make one more stop at the grocery store to buy food for the next two-to-three days. Food shopping would consist of regular staples for typical meals like spaghetti with a package of tuna and spaghetti sauce (preferable Newman's Own because it comes in a plastic bottle that is lighter than the glass sauces). I also bought some dried fruit, bagels for breakfast, some cashew nuts, and the much needed (but much-maligned) bag of white powdered doughnuts, one of my go-to biking staples.

I flew through the grocery store in less than 20 minutes, and it was time to get serious. I had less than 4 hours to go the last 40 miles before it would to start to get dark. I knew this was a concern because Pfeifer Big Sur State Park included lots of large trees such as redwoods that would block out the sun and get the campground darker sooner than the ocean beaches west of the park. I made one last check of my ACA map that I had on my phone to see exactly how far I had to go and what kind of elevation was in front of me. Past experience told me it was always a safe assumption that my average speed would be about 10 miles per hour, whether there were hills or not. This average would include photo stops, water breaks, stoplights, etc. While I might go down hills anywhere from 15-to-30 miles per hour and ride uphill at 4-to-9 miles per hour, I would average 10 miles per hour.

Big Sur is one of the most beautiful places in the world to drive a car or ride a bike. Many car commercials – and a recent motorcycle insurance commercial – have been filmed along the Big Sur due to its beauty. In March 2019, I got lucky because California had been experiencing a great deal of rain, so the ordinarily golden grasses were very green, and this made the picturesque landscape pop even more. It also helped that it was very sunny out as I biked up and down the hills of the Big Sur.

Of course, a true landmark on this day would be stopping at the Bixby Bridge. The roaring ocean below and the beauty of the bridge connecting the two hills was breathtaking. While the cars and trucks were driving beside me, I couldn't help but be in wonderment of riding over such a beautiful bridge that I have seen in many TV commercials. But once I got over the bridge, I had a challenging hill to go up. I put my bike in its granny gear and slowly made my way up the mountain. I like going uphill because of the challenge and my curiosity about what beautiful scenery I'll behold once I get to the top of the hill. One of the best parts of biking down the West Coast of the United States is that you mostly have the Pacific Ocean on your right-hand side. The stiff breeze will cool you off, the sound of the crashing waves is refreshing, the vistas you see are glorious, and the fact you can see down the coast gives you anticipation that you have a spectacular bike ride ahead. Of course, it is a little scarier riding down the hill, knowing there are many cars, trucks, and RVs, also looking at the beautiful views and hopefully recognizing there is a biker in front of them. I found that drivers in California were great to bikers. I had very few, if any, drivers honk at me, and if anything, they were more than courteous and operated safely near me.

Biking the Big Sur was a surreal experience, for it certainly is a beautiful place; however, I did feel I had a time crunch as I didn't want to be setting up camp in the dark on the first day. I hadn't set up my tent since I hiked around the Tetons on the Teton Crest Trail six months earlier. I felt like I still did not have my camping mojo yet, so having as much sunlight to make mistakes would be a prudent thing to do.

While biking on my first day, I discovered an unwritten rule about my psyche. The rule supposes that once I am getting close to my destination, time slows down, and it seems like I will never get there. It is weird, the first fifty miles seemed to go by fast as I was excited to be finally on my bike taking this great adventure, the views were spectacular, and I already felt comfortable biking among the hundreds of vehicles also enjoying the scenery. You could say I was in "flow" as I never noticed the miles melting away as I was off in some fantasy land induced by steady exercise and beautiful scenery. However, in the last two miles, I would get something that I would refer to as the "two-mile syndrome." It seemed the last two miles felt like two hundred miles. I think the problem was that my state of flow stopped by me beginning to think. By accessing the reasoning center of my brain, I would start to realize I was tired, hungry, the uphill portion of the road would bother me, and I would start to get impatient because all of a sudden, I couldn't wait to finish. I had been pushing my body for so long in a state of bliss that it never dawned on me that I was tired and hungry, especially because it was the first day. The "two-mile syndrome" would become a recurring theme throughout my ride.

While it seemed like an eternity (but it wasn't in reality), I finally biked into the Pfeifer Big Sur State Park. I had been to this park a few times in the past, but the sight of the big, beautiful redwood trees always takes my breath away. The smell of the trees, the shade, and the beauty that was the park felt very satisfying.

I biked into the hiker/biker campground, and I was the only camper there as it was still early season. Once I found the levelest ground, I immediately took out my tent and started setting up just in case it started to rain, at the same time, I lit my camp stove so I could cook dinner. I did lock my bike to a tree for safety. Since it was getting late, I decided to eat a ready-made meal I bought at REI, Kung Pao Chicken, as all I needed to do was add water. The Kung

Pao Chicken had two servings, but it proved to be an excellent single serving for one hungry biker.

As I went to bed after my first day of riding, I was excited that I stretched myself to get to the Big Sur. I felt great. I also was excited to see what tomorrow would bring, considering it had started raining and the forecast was for showers. My goal for the next day was to camp just south of the Hearst Castle, past San Simeon. It would be 65 miles and 9,300 feet of elevation gain, which meant biking up and down big hills all day. It was getting real now.

## Day 2 – (65 miles) Pfeifer Big Sur State Park to San Simeon State Park Campground

*"That which does not kill us makes us stronger."*
*– Friedrich Nietzsche*

I set my alarm for 6 AM, knowing that I would be waking up in the dark. From my experience on my first bike touring trip down the west coast a year and half earlier, I got more enjoyment out of my ride by riding as soon as I could see in front of me because there was no traffic, little-to-no wind, no other bikers, more wild animals running around, and lots of peace and tranquility. I self-labeled my morning routine to those who would listen as "bike touring using the McGinty Method". The McGinty Method entailed waking up in the dark, breaking down your camp while eating something simple like a bagel, energy bar, or my ever-present white powdered donuts, immediately biking thirty miles while you were still half asleep and then after you completed thirty or so miles, you eat a large breakfast with lots of hot coffee which actually wakes you up completely. The breakfast and coffee give you the energy and caffeine to have a regular bike touring day of fifty to sixty miles which seems very doable; however, the difference is that you already did thirty miles plus the fifty to sixty miles you are about to complete equals a very doable eighty to ninety miles per day without a great deal of struggle. With this method, you will complete your ride in the early afternoon without biking in the hottest part of the day. The McGinty Method worked well on my first tour, where I would average biking 68 miles per day. My goal on my bike across the US was to average about eighty miles per day by the time I hit Florida. I did recognize the first week I would slowly get my biking legs used to the mileage, but I was confident that once I hit the deserts and rural areas of Texas, I would start averaging eighty-plus miles per day using the McGinty Method and even have a few hundred-plus days. We'd see.

My morning routine consisted of setting my phone alarm 30 minutes before the first light would glimmer. Once my alarm went off, I would give myself 60 seconds in my sleeping bag to solidify my game plan, especially since this was my first morning. Once I had my plan, I would bolt out of my warm sleeping bag and start putting on my bike clothes, stuffing my sleeping bag in my carrying bag, and roll up my Thermarest. To add more immediacy and challenge, I would try to pack up the inside of my tent before my morning urgent urination, as this would get me moving even faster. It usually took me about 25 minutes from getting out of my warm sleeping bag to being on the road toward my destination in the morning. I never cook anything in the morning when touring and I eat a bagel while taking my tent down. Since it was still early in my trip, I had plenty of fat reserves as I loaded up on hamburgers, steaks, ice cream, and other high-calorie foods to gain an extra 6 pounds before I left because I knew I was going to lose a significant amount of weight by the time I hit Florida. During my last bike trip from Longview, Washington to Monterey, I biked just over a thousand miles in 16 days and lost 16 pounds even though I ate like a horse. I was confident going forward I would eat all kinds of wrong, high caloric food that would give an average person a premature heart attack. It would turn out that I would be quite prophetic.

On this first morning of the ride, I felt great as I was excited to bike down the Big Sur. In the spring of 2017, I was not able to complete my bike trip from Longview to Los Angeles, because of mudslides along the Big Sur that closed the Pacific Coast Highway at the Pfeifer Big Sur State Park. In spring 2019, the highway reopened.

The Big Sur is a rugged 91-mile stretch of California's Central Coast between Carmel and San Simeon. It is bordered to the east by the Santa Lucia Mountains and to the west by the Pacific Ocean. The road is very winding, with steep hills, two narrow lanes, and usually had foggy, misty weather, especially in the morning.

Once I got out on the road, I knew I was in for a challenging day as the road was wet from the rain the night before. There was also a thick fog, it was humid, and my day started with a big hill. Intellectually I know I should start my ride a little cold and not overdress; however, I still must have been soft because I had all my warm clothes on because it was raw, wet, and I was feeling cold. Starting with all my clothes on was a newbie mistake as it only took about a mile before I was sweating bullets. I had to stop to find somewhere to lean my bike, so I could disrobe, which meant taking off my rain pants, fleece, warm hat, and full-fingered gloves. While it was still foggy and misty, just having my bike shorts, a short-sleeve shirt, a waterproof raincoat, and half-fingered gloves felt good. I was now warmed up and ready to tackle the day.

Once I got to the top of the hill, the fog didn't help with me seeing what I can imagine was a beautiful vista. It was a bit disappointing that I could not see much, but I felt lucky the day before to see the Big Sur in all its glory with cliffs, beautiful bridges, deserted beaches, sea stacks, and lots of crashing waves. Part of my desire to ride further than I initially planned was being strategic in knowing that it could rain the next day, so I wanted to experience as much of the Big Sur in good weather as I could and yesterday fit the bill judging from the beautiful pictures I had gathered. Today would be a different story. However, as the day went on, the weather would clear up.

Biking the Big Sur is like a big roller coaster. Up five hundred feet and then down five hundred feet. It was fun to blast down the hill, but it seemed like my day was spent mostly going uphill because I would go uphill at four to six miles per hour and downhill fifteen to thirty although during the early part of the morning when the roads were especially wet I would also go slow on the downhills because I didn't want to crash due to the damp pavement.

While the views, smells, and sounds of the Big Sur were thrilling, the most anticipated area I looked forward to biking was the area known as the "mother of all landslides." The landslide was a mile south of Gorda. The 2017 landslide was made up of six billion tons of rock and dirt which took out a quarter-mile section of Highway 1. It closed the highway for almost two years before it was considered safe to travel. The landslide was so massive that instead of the usual removing the dirt and rock on the road with bulldozers, authorities decided that since the landslide created 13 new acres of land area they would build a new road on top of the old road.

During my last bike tour, I had to stop in Monterey because of the road closures; however, I would later talk to another bike tourist who told me in 2017 he biked down the west coast and skirted both closed sections of the highway. At the first closure on Highway 1, he carried his bike over the damaged bridge that was closed to the public near Pfeifer Big Sur State Park and then when he got to Gorda and the massive landslide, he waited for the security guard who was posted at the landslide to get off of work at 5 pm, and then he walked his bike over the landslide to get to the other side of it so he could continue his bike journey south to San Diego. Yikes, that is a whole different level of crazy!

After going up and down hills to the tune of 9,300 feet in sixty miles, I reached San Simeon, where I went into town to relax and get a coffee at the local touristy coffee shop. It felt wonderful to stop and rest. I wanted to spread out my tent so it could dry it off, but I didn't see any appropriate areas to spread it out without it bringing a lot of attention and looking awkward. I drank my $1 coffee and did some people watching.

Once I left San Simeon, I rolled onto Highway 1. The highway in this area was flat. There were lots of sea lions and seals bathing on various local beaches you can see off the highway. The sounds of the crashing waves and honking sea lions warmed my soul as much as the sun and different wildflowers along the road. Unfortunately, less than two miles from my campground, I all of a sudden "bonked." Bonking is when your body gives out on you and you cannot ride your bike further. I was light-headed, dizzy, lost all energy, and needed to stop and lie on the ground. I found a road sign to lean my bike against that had a grassy patch in front of it I could lie down on. I surveyed the area for any snakes before I rested in the grass. It was like my power plant gave out. It was only day two, and biking more than sixty miles up and down hills was hard on my body, so it let me know what it thought of my athletic challenge by shutting down. It freaked me out a bit, but I drank some water, rested up, and as sickening as it sounds, I ate a full bag of white powdered donuts. I thought the donuts should at least temporarily recharge my engine enough to fuel my effort to bike the two miles down the road to the campground. After 20 minutes of lying down, drinking water, and stuffing 1,400 calories of white powdered donuts into my gullet, I felt much better. I completed the last two miles with vigor and was happy to be ending the day.

Once I paid the $10 at the entrance to San Simeon Creek Campground, I biked over to the hiker/biker section and found it to be waterlogged. A couple of other older bike tourists told me that they made the executive decision to move their tent to a car camping spot since the campground was not full. I ended up doing the same as it made no sense to camp in the wet area with my already damp camp equipment. The first thing I did was place my tent on top of various picnic tables so that the warm setting sun would dry my tent, rainfly, groundsheet, and anything else that was wet. While my gear was drying, I got to know my fellow bike tourists who were older road warriors still enjoying bike touring even though they were in their mid to upper sixties. They were both married, and their wives were fully supportive of their travels together. One of the gentlemen was a prostate cancer survivor and was still riding his bike with a specially designed seat that looked like a half-moon, so only his butt cheeks rested on the seat. Both gentlemen were a joy to talk with. They had biked and hiked in many areas of the US that I had been myself, including Alaska. I did detect that the both of them seemed to be bike touring purist as they believed a person completing a journey such as the Pacific Coast Bicycle Route or the Southern Tier should ride the whole way without once walking any sections. This discussion came about because I, unfortunately, told them I was not one to forego a "walking break" if my psyche or body needed it. I believed as long as your trip is 100% human-powered, it is a good trip, and a little break was good for the body and soul. "Rubbish," they said, and believed a person is cheating if they don't fully ride the whole tour. Their resolve made me feel like a wimp. We eventually agreed to disagree, but I thought these two older gentlemen were bigger biking "bad-asses" than myself. Full disclosure: I still took periodic "walking breaks" throughout my 3,411-mile journey and felt great doing it!

## Day 3 – (40 miles) San Simeon State Park Campground to San Luis Obispo

*"There will always be serendipity involved in discovery."*
*– Jeff Bezos*

I woke up early after a great sleep. I was off again as soon as I could see in front of me. It was tranquil, and I had Highway 1 to myself. I must have been exhausted as I slept like a rock; however, I felt I was still recovering from bonking the day before, and my body was still trying to adjust to the rigors of bike touring.

Today I had an open-ended goal. I knew I had a friend of a friend I could visit in San Luis Obispo (SLO), but since I was well ahead of my original schedule, SLO was only forty miles away from where I would start, and that was a short riding day. My goal was to try to ride seventy to eighty miles per day, especially since I was out of the mountains and into flatter lands. I was considering stopping for breakfast in Cambria because I remember having a great breakfast there 17 years earlier, but since it wasn't even 7am, I figured nowhere was open. As I biked by Cambria on Highway 1, it seemed a lot more crowded and built up since the last time I was there, so I decided my one bagel could hold me over until I hit Morro Bay.

Before I got to Morro Bay, I stopped at a cute small town named Cayucos. It was a little touristy but sleepy before 8 AM. I decided to get off Highway 1 to check out the town and follow the bike trail. It ended up being good and bad. It was good in that the town was appealing and I considered finding a breakfast place, but I decided to wait until Morro Bay which would be the magic thirty miles away; it turned out bad because the bike trail turned out to be a local bike trail that guided me two miles off track to a dead end at a local beach. Getting lost is a part of bike touring, but even adding a mile or two to an already big day is draining. Since leaving Monterey, I did not have to think as the route was strictly on Highway 1, but periodically, the route would exit Highway 1, and this is where a biker can easily take a wrong turn and get lost. Going forward, I would get lost many times.

Once I got my equilibrium back and was back on Highway 1, I biked as fast as I could to Morro Bay because I could feel that I was starting to get very hungry. I have to admit I was a bit surprised how spread out and crowded Morro Bay was as compared to Cayucos. A theme that would arise throughout my bike tour was I always seemed excited to get to a bigger town or a city, but once I got there, I couldn't wait to leave and preferred the tranquility and perceived friendliness of the smaller towns.

It is funny I did not see anywhere I was interested in having breakfast, so I took out my phone and googled the nearest, yes you guessed it, McDonalds. Once at Mickie D's, I had a sausage egg McMuffin with no cheese and a medium coffee before I continued on my journey toward Morro Bay State Park.

The biking in Morro Bay State Park and the surrounding area was beautiful as it was very green. The fields were so green that I couldn't tell whether I was in California or Ireland. While enjoying the beautiful green fields, I stopped to look at a hawk that was less than 5 feet from me on a post. I took its picture, and while it looked at me, it was not afraid of me. I left it alone and continued to marvel at the beautiful landscape before me.

As I was getting closer to San Luis Obispo, I started having an internal debate whether I should forego going to SLO because I found a short cut that would cut five miles from my ride and get me closer to Guadalupe where I possibly could camp behind a fire station and get a shower at the station. It would also get me closer to my next day destination and save me from having a very long ninety-mile day. However, I like to be a man of my word, so I made a split decision to head to SLO to see Keith Pellemeier. My initial plan was to see Keith for a cup of coffee and then head to Guadalupe.

As I started toward SLO, a headwind seemed to suck whatever energy I had out of me. It didn't help that once I got to SLO, there were lots of red lights, traffic, and my cell phone, which I set to show Keith's house on Google Maps, was inside my handlebar bag, but I could not hear the directions because of all the traffic noise. When I finally got to Keith's house, I was a mess. I had to calm myself down and be grateful I got to see a friendly face.

While it seemed a little uncomfortable to stop by someone's house who you never met; however, once I met Keith Pellemeier, he was super friendly. Whatever stress I was under just seemed to melt away. He had unique energy, just like our mutual friend John Mason.

Keith poured me some coffee and made me a sandwich from his garden. I am always appreciative of any healthy food because I can't seem to make any good food choices for myself as my choices usual include McDonalds, Cheetos, and white powdered donuts. Initially, I had planned to only stay for one cup of coffee and conversation. Keith was very engaging and let it be known I could stay or go, that he was okay with both. I was impressed with his openness. I felt I arrived at Keith's place, a wounded warrior, as I was struggling on the bike, but I was feeling very comfortable in his house. The death knell of me continuing on my journey that day was the pouring of the second cup of coffee and more conversation. I would label the turn of events "second cup of coffee syndrome." A second cup of coffee would make me relax to the point of no return. During my bike trip, I would be tempted by it often, and occasionally would succumb to its charm. After the second cup of coffee with Keith, I resigned myself to stay the night. We would have a great rest of the day as we went hot tubbing, took a tour of SLO, ate dinner, drank wine, and told hilarious stories about our mutual friend John Mason. I also got to sleep in a comfortable bed. While I only ended up riding forty miles that day, the respite of hanging with Keith boosted my spirits and helped heal my body and mind so that I could continue my journey. In the end, I am grateful Keith hosted me, and I appreciated his hospitality. I almost didn't stop by, but serendipity brought us together, and I was better for it.

### *Day 4 – (90 miles) San Luis Obispo to Refugio State Beach Campground*

> *"Gratitude is the fairest blossom that springs from the soul."*
> *– Henry Ward Beecher*

I woke up very early again, and Keith had coffee on. I refused a second cup of coffee. It was hard to leave Keith and SLO, but the show must go on as I had a ninety-mile day to get to Refugio State Park. However, the short riding day, good dinner, and hospitality seemed to provide a boost to my energy plant, and I blasted out of SLO like a man on a mission.

The early morning provides beautiful riding as the air is cool, and there seems to be a promise to the day that it was going to be a good one. I loved the fact that the area was flat and enjoyed biking through the Pismo Beach area. I remember the guys I met at the campsite in San Simeon said they were staying in Pismo last night, so I thought it would be cool if I would bump into them again. It made for a good intellectual exercise to look for them, and it indeed passed some time; however, I never did see them, and it could be that we were on separate schedules as I like to start biking early and they started when they felt like it, as they only did forty-to-fifty miles per day.

Once I got out of the Pismo Beach area, I started passing large farms and farming communities. I started taking notice that strangers, in this case, mostly farmhands would wave and say a friendly "Hi" to me as I biked by where they were working. I was surprised at the gesture but would wave as enthusiastically back to them. I thought it a bit strange, but the story I came up to myself was that perhaps they appreciated that I had the freedom to bike freely while they had to toil. It certainly made me feel grateful that I had the opportunity to do what I was doing.

At one point, I was in a severe need to urinate, and there was so much open farmland and cars driving by that there was nowhere readily available that I could take care of business. There were no stores, no bathrooms, but I did see a small overpass, so in my desperation, I stopped my bike and leaned it on the guard rail. I wanted to run under the bridge, relieve myself, and then get back to my bike as soon as possible. I was always suspicious of someone stealing my bike, stealing something on my bike, or even attracting the negative attention of a nice, fully loaded bike out in the open unlocked. As I ran down the embankment to pee under the bridge, I was dumbfounded when I saw what appeared to be the furniture and belongings of at least a couple of families who lived under the bridge. There were even toys for kids, but there was no one there at the time I arrived, which made me think they were probably out in the fields and the kids, perhaps in school. However, I was appalled that there were families in America living under a bridge. I quickly reversed course and ended up peeing in the line of traffic because I didn't want to pee on the people's home boundaries. The experience was a reminder of how privileged I am. Others do what they have to do to survive and make a better life.

Once I got back on the bike, I spent the next few hours processing what I just saw as I continued to roll through farms and farming communities. I ended up taking a quick break in Guadalupe as the sun was getting hot and I needed something to hold me over until lunch. Unfortunately, I ended up taking a Gatorade break with a bag of extra-hot Cheetos. Not exactly full of nutrition, but the fat and sugar were welcoming.

The next few hours were a blur as I biked like a madman, lost in thought, soaking up the sun, and doing my best not to get lost between large farms. The traffic started to get busy as I headed to the coast, and I noticed again within five miles of reaching my destination the energy plant in my body was beginning to waver, especially since I just biked 85 miles.

It was a great feeling to finally get off the highway and bike downhill toward the beach where I would be pitching my tent. I would pay only $10 for a hiker/biker site. Just as I got to the front gate, I saw a half dozen turkey vultures feasting on some roadkill. It amazes me that such a large bird with beautiful feathers was rather ugly looking due to their skinny head and neck. Also, since they are scavengers, they do not have the highest reputation. They also seemed to be skittish for a sturdy looking raptor because as I got close to them, they would all fly away but not too far. As soon as I passed, they would soar right back to the roadkill.

At the beach, I had difficulty pitching my tent because the wind was fierce. It must have been blowing thirty-plus mile per hour gusts as my tent almost went sailing into the Pacific Ocean. My strategy in setting up my tent was to stake my groundsheet first and then slowly add my tent, poles, and then the toughest of all to set up in the wind, the rain fly. After ten minutes of wrestling with the tent, it was up, and I could add my gear to weigh the tent down. I then added protection by adding several large rocks on to my tent stakes to keep the tent from blowing into the ocean.

It ended up being so windy that I cooked dinner by the restrooms. I had my spaghetti cooking as I was taking a shower. While in the shower, I first noticed I had the hot spots of saddle sores, which are bad for someone bike touring. Saddle sores are like blisters on your ass, usually caused by friction, that if they burst, they could become infected and lead to severe medical issues. During my first bike tour of the Pacific Coast in 2017, I ended up getting severe saddle sores on my last day as I biked 99 miles from Half Moon Bay Beach to Monterey. I had run out of chamois crème, and the cheap Noxzema I was using was useless because I was so sweaty that after 70 miles, the Noxzema evaporated and didn't help with any friction. My saddle sores were so bad that I could not sit on my bike seat for the last ten miles. I had to stand and pedal the whole way to Monterey. It ended

up a good thing that I had to end my bike ride in Monterey due to the landslides because I would not have been able to continue without possibly seriously harming my health.

On day 4 of my ride, I was very concerned to be dealing with saddle sores because I knew if they burst, my bike trip would likely be over. My only comfort was that I had a big saddle sore on my right butt cheek and nothing yet on my left butt cheek. I figured the reason I had the saddle sores was because of my old bike shorts had lost their integrity (kind of like how you need to replace running shoes after 500 miles because your feet begin to hurt). I realized I needed medicine for my sores, but currently, I was out in the middle of nowhere, and my next shopping opportunity was twenty-five miles away in Santa Barbara. I was seriously concerned, but at least I had a plan to get medicine the next day and to start the road to recovery. I was determined not to go home because of a zit on my ass.

## Day 5 – (80 miles) Refugio State Beach Campground to Sycamore Canyon Campground

*"Being challenged in life is inevitable; being defeated is optional."*
*– Roger Crawford*

I didn't get a great sleep because I kept thinking about my saddle sores and was strategizing about what I needed to do to take care of them.

I got up at my standard time and left as the sun was coming up. The saddle sore on my right butt cheek was still bothering me, so I biked to Santa Barbara on my left butt cheek. I thought this would be the right short-term solution but not a good long-term solution. It was only twenty-five miles to Santa Barbara, so I felt confident I would make it without bursting any saddle sores. There was little traffic on the highway, and the ride into Santa Barbara was smooth. I found the University of California Santa Barbara campus very lovely, although I kept getting lost biking through it because I find it hard to keep track of bike trails on my ACA map. Eventually, I just found it easier to bike with my phone in my hand so I could check my progress and direction when there were a lot of tricky turns.

Once I got into Santa Barbara, I headed straight to the CVS drug store. The night before, I did some research on how other bikers have dealt with their saddle sores. It appeared the best way to deal with saddle sores was to treat it like a zit, so I got some Neutrogena Acne treatment soap, some zit cream with benzoyl peroxide, and a super lubricant called Bug Balm. My little regimen would clear out the bacteria with a good wash, the cream would dry up the zits that already formed, and the bug balm would be a super lubricant to reduce friction in my seat area. I already had chamois butt cream, which I would also use.

I was relieved to notice that Santa Barbara had an REI, but it did not open until 10 am, so I went to have breakfast at McDonalds. I noticed a lot of homeless and perhaps meth addicts in front of McDonalds, so I thought it best to lock my bike. I also wanted to take my bike shorts off so I could wash my saddle-sore area in the McDonalds bathroom, spread some of my acne cream, and put on a loose pair of shorts so that my butt area could breathe better and dry out. I then went back outside to my locked bike to put my bike shorts nasty side out and spread out on top of my dry bag and panniers to be a kind of barrier and deterrent to anyone wanting to see what was under the bike shorts. It was a bit crude but practical. To get to my stuff, a would-be thief would have to touch my nasty bike shorts. Good luck with that!

At this point, I was famished and was very focused on getting in line and ordering my meal. As I was headed to order, someone noticed my bike clothes and started talking to me about how they biked across the US twenty years ago. The guy was enthusiastic and excited to talk to me; however, I was in a bit of a predicament because I was starving and was still suffering angst about my saddle sores that I didn't want to talk to anyone at that moment. I tried to be friendly. I'm sure my body language communicated more than my words. At one point, the guy got his meal, wished me luck, and ate alone. I should have been more responsive, but I was a little delirious due to my hunger. Once I finished my breakfast, I took the initiative to talk with my fellow biker, and I apologized for not communicating more with him earlier. I tried to explain, but he said he understood. I then had a great conversation with him about his bike trip. He told me the best place to ride a bike was California, as everyone was courteous to bikers (which I found true), and the worst area was Florida (which turned out to not be accurate in my experience as Alabama was the worst). I also asked if he ever suffered from saddle sores, and he said he did not. He said what he did to combat saddle sores was he would bike uphill standing up and would "mash" (stand and pedal) every five-to-ten minutes for two minutes to get circulation in the seat area. He was confident this method would help alleviate saddle sore issues. I thanked him for his time and liked his idea about mashing.

I was feeling better about my saddle sores as I had medication on them, a couple of new strategies to get more air circulating in my seat area, and was now heading over to REI to buy new bike shorts. At REI, I had a choice of expensive bike shorts or cheaper, basic bike shorts. At this point, I was so desperate to get rid of my saddle sores I considered the expensive shorts if they were better for saddle sores. However, while trying on the expensive bike shorts, I couldn't get them over my legs, and there were going to be so tight that my legs would turn blue. Also, the actual butt pad seemed smaller because I am sure it was to cut weight. The basic pair appeared to have a nicer, bigger butt pad, and they were comfortable to put on and wear. This decision was a no brainer and was better for my wallet.

For the rest of the day, my saddle sores, while on the mend, were still on my mind. I rode the rest of the day on my left butt cheek. Every time I had an extended break, I would take my bike shorts off and relax in my loose, fast-drying nylon gym shorts. I also placed my bike shorts inside out to dry in the sun on my bike. I even biked a fifteen mile stretch with just my gym shorts so that I could air out my seat area. I biked a lot standing up as I cruised along the beaches of Ventura County and gawked in awe at the super-bloom of wildflowers displayed on the hillsides. It was beautiful and hot outside, but my saddle sores took much of my attention.

By the end of the day, I biked 78 miles on my left butt cheek and was feeling confident that I could overcome my saddle sores. However, the next few days would make or break the trip.

I arrived at Sycamore Canyon Campground, at Point Magu State Park. At camp, I was again at a hiker/biker site and noticed there was only one other tent in the area. It was still considered early to be biking down the Pacific coast, so I hadn't seen any other bike tourists in my five days. It turned out the other camper was a German guy named Jan-Casper, who quit his job in Vancouver, British Columbia because he wanted a new challenge. His new challenge was to run from Vancouver to San Diego. He was averaging thirty miles per day, and he was pulling a small trailer behind him with sixty pounds of gear. He had been on the road for about three months and was studying Spanish because he was thinking of continuing to Chile. He was taking a couple of days at the camp to rest and regroup. I was amazed at what he was doing. His adventure certainly seemed crazier than my trip. He was a great guy to talk to and was full of positive energy. I wished him the best of luck whereever he ended up on his adventure. It was not unusual to meet another adventurer, whether on a bike or not, who was attempting a crazier or more extended trip than I was doing. It always inspired me!

### Day 6 – (94 miles) Sycamore Canyon Campground to Corona Del Mar, California

> *"All that glitters is not gold, all who wander are not lost."*
> *– J.R. R. Tolkien*

The quiet was deafening as I tip-toed out of the campsite in the dark because I woke up early. I was excited to get started. Today I would be biking to beaches I always dreamed of biking down including the bike paths on Santa Monica, Venice Beach, Manhattan Beach, and Redondo Beach.

Once I got on to Highway 1, there was no one on the usually busy highway, and there was a light fog. The rising sun began burning the mist off as I entered Malibu. Whenever I am in Malibu, I always look around extra diligently to see if I see anyone famous. In the three times I have been to Malibu I have never seen anyone well-known, but it doesn't stop me from thinking this could be the day. Looking for famous people is one of those mind games I like to play while on my bike to stimulate it with different thoughts other than thinking about logistics, food, and my saddle-sore situation.

After biking twenty-five miles and having a big breakfast at the Malibu McDonalds, I noticed the traffic was getting a little busier on Highway 1 as it was just after 8 am. I was hoping to hit Will Rogers State Beach before 8 am because I know the bike paths can get crowded, especially being it was Saturday. With my new energy from breakfast, I quickly rode the last eight miles to Will Rogers State Beach, riding confidently with all the high-end cars headed to Santa Monica.

It was another surreal moment as I biked into Will Rogers State Beach and onto the bike path that would lead me to Santa Monica Beach Pier. I was a year and a half late, but the feeling was just as exciting even with the path a little more crowded than I used to like it when rollerblading many years ago. The trail was just as smooth as I remember it. The sun was hot, the beautiful people were out in force, lots of gung-ho exercisers as well as those just trying to lose a few pounds, and the glistening sandy beach was as glorious as ever. I felt an exceptional warmth as I biked the path. All kinds of great memories from the past came to mind. Venice Beach was starting to get crowded, and I was glad to finish the Venice section when I did. While on Venice Beach, I did take a quick look to see who was playing basketball and if any monsters were lifting weights. I did not see anyone famous. I also passed the old Italian restaurant my girlfriend Ann and I went to over ten years earlier. I always laugh because every thirty minutes, the staff would have the patrons join in the singing of "That's Amore." The singing of the song had an impact on me as I can still remember it many years later.

With Santa Monica and Venice Beaches completed, I was now excited to bike down the bike paths to Redondo Beach. Again, the well-maintained bike trails did not disappoint, and it was prototypical California with lots of sun, surfer dudes, and California girls. The riding was flat, smooth, and filled with lots of eye candy. The only ugly part was biking by a power plant on the other side of the highway, but I guess they have to put power plants somewhere to power a massive city like Los Angeles.

I never did stop at the beach to take a dip in the water or tan myself because that is not me. People who know me know that I do not like to jump in the water. Friends also know of the story when I spent ten days in Hawaii and did not get in the water once. To many, it was a blasphemous act, but when you have a fear of water, not feeling pressured to jump in is relieving. I must say though I love looking at the water and appreciate the power of the oceans. I, for most of my life, lived on the east or west coast and like nothing better than walking, biking, hiking, or rollerblading near the water. Just do not ask me to jump in it.

Once my beach tour was over, the part of my ride that I dreaded was upon me. I had to now cut through the city of Los Angeles and, more specifically, Torrance and Carson. My first ignorant thought was that the areas were gang havens, and the traffic was probably thick and terrible. However, I was lucky it was Saturday morning, but there was still a good deal of traffic, the drivers were courteous for the most part (only one person honked at me), and the roads included some bike lanes. I didn't see any gang bangers, and some of the side streets I went down were quite lovely. The whole fifteen-plus miles I rode through Torrance and Carson wasn't as bad as I thought. Throughout my ride through Los Angeles, I kept anticipating a terrible section that never materialized. It reminded me of the Stoic philosophy technique to have negative visualizations so that you can prepare yourself for a bad situation and not be disappointed. Due to my negative thoughts of biking through L.A., I had meager expectations of my ride, but my journey turned out to be much better than I expected, although I wouldn't want to do it again.

Once I was through L.A., I then rode along the aqueducts before hitting the Long Beach bike paths. Long Beach was more beautiful than I expected as the paths seemed new. I got to view the Queen Mary, which looked rather puny next to a multideck modern ocean liner.

Today was a day of riding beach after beach as Seal Beach, Huntington Beach and Newport Beach were to follow. It was a beautiful sunny day, and I could feel my legs, ears, and face burning because I had yet to buy any sunscreen. There was a gentle ocean breeze to keep me slightly cool, and riding while people watching was fantastic. California certainly had lots of beautiful sights.

After biking by the beach for over eight hours, I finally reached the ferry that would take me to Balboa Island. I had lived on the tiny island of Balboa thirty years earlier and had fond memories of playing basketball at the small basketball court near the ferry terminal and walking the path around the beautiful island. The island has a lot of hummingbirds and had a real peaceful charm to it. Since I was arriving on a Saturday, the traffic off the ferry was a nightmare. I couldn't maneuver my bike on the road or sidewalk because of the hordes of cars and people. There appeared to be some car show going on as all the cars were vintage sports cars and were clogging the island streets. After a quarter-mile of gridlock, I headed over to my old abode on Little Balboa Island. I stopped by my old house where I lived with a roommate named Kim in the maid's quarters in the back of the house. The house was as I remembered it. I only lived there for less than three months, but the memories were wonderful because it was the chance for a young twenty-something to experience California living. Good times!

Tonight, I would have my first Warmshower experience. Warmshowers is a non-profit organization and community of people who host other adventurers, usually people biking long distances. They typically provide a shower and a place to sleep. Your sleeping arrangement could be a couch, blow-up bed, spare bed, or something else. Sometimes they may do your laundry, cook for you, drive you for errands, or even give you useful local tips or shortcut directions. It is a great community filled with wonderfully, hospitable people who frequently have tremendous travel stories to share.

My Warmshower hosts were a couple who were incredible adventurers themselves. They traveled all over the world on a shoestring and had fabulous stories. They loved hosting travelers because they meet interesting people, and it gave them a chance to give back to a community that had given them so much in the past.

As soon as I arrived at my host site, they gave me a beer and we got to know each other. It was a very comfortable atmosphere and I didn't feel out of place with my hosts. They seemed like long-lost friends even though I just met them. After taking a much-needed shower, I ended up sleeping in the den on a futon on the floor. It was a restful sleep, and a remarkable first Warmshower stay.

### Day 7 – (96 miles) Corona Del Mar to San Diego

> *"The end of one stage is only the beginning of another. Any dangers overcome are the necessary preparation to do better on the next stage."*
> – Paulo Coelho

I slipped out of my host site as quietly as I could so as not to wake my hosts. The light was starting to sprout when I hit Highway 1 towards Laguna Beach. It was a beautiful early morning ride to Laguna as the air smelled clean and fresh. There were lots of birds flying overhead, and I was reveling in the warm feeling of being grateful for my Warmshower hosts.

Today was going to be another excellent beach biking day. However, my bike was making some harsh sounding noises coming from my bottom bracket, and my pedaling power seemed inefficient. I thought it was important that I get my bike checked ASAP. I wondered if any bike shops were open on Sundays and whether they would even consider doing an emergency repair. It was essential to get the bike fixed because once I headed out of San Diego, my choice of bike shops would dwindle. It would be a terrible situation to have my bike break down in the middle of the desert, which would be the worst-case scenario I feared.

After my first break at Laguna Beach, I realized I lost my light nylon running shorts. Later, I realized I left them at my host site. I was not having a good day as I loved those shorts, and my bike was in bad shape. My thoughts started going negative as I wondered if I would have to take a "zero" day in San Diego to get my bike fixed and I also began to catastrophize about having bike problems while in the middle of the desert. I even briefly thought about whether I should bike to San Diego and call it good. I was a mess looking for an open bike shop on a Sunday morning.

As I biked into San Clemente, I noticed there was a bike shop near the bike route, but it did not open until 10 am. I arrived in San Clemente at 9:30 but thought it was worth my time to wait the thirty minutes because the noise coming out of the bike was getting worse. Just as the shop opened, I headed straight to the mechanic and asked if they do emergency repairs for someone who is touring across the country. While the mechanic was a bit busy with other customers, he told me he would take a look and see what he could do for me. He took my bike out for a quick spin and realized the problem. I needed a new bearing in my bottom bracket. At first, he said he didn't have the specific part I needed; however, he checked his storage room and happened to have a particular order that a customer never picked up; that was the exact bearing required. How lucky is that?

The mechanic was excellent and a true professional. As I was talking to him, I had mentioned that I was having a bad morning as I lost my shorts. Without hesitation, he quickly found and gave me some nice shorts that had been lying around the shop for free. I was super grateful as I certainly needed them. By 11 am, the mechanic replaced the bearing on my bottom bracket and put on a new chain. The bike ran like new, and I was much appreciative of their prompt service. The cost was reasonable. I was not soaked like I thought I might be in my vulnerable state.

I continued south with a big smile on my face as I thought my karma must be very positive as at 9:45 am I was stressing big time, but by 11 am my bike was fixed, and I had a decent pair of shorts.

With my renewed attitude and what seemed like a faster bike, I was excited to stretch myself and make it to San Diego. I wanted to do the ceremonial dipping of my back tire, signifying the start of my cross America bike ride.

My next challenge was how I was going to bike through Camp Pendleton, a United States Marine Corps Training Depot. While I could probably jump on the very busy Interstate 5 (I-5); however, I decided to continue south on the Old Pacific Highway I was on until I could go no further. It wasn't long before I hit a park ranger manning a station. Initially, he said if I wanted to bypass Camp Pendleton, I would need to backtrack five miles and jump on I-5. Backtracking to a bike tourist is always to be avoided. I pleaded with the ranger to let me through because I did not want to backtrack, and I heard there was a way, through a hole in the fence, I can go to get through Camp Pendleton. His resolve must have melted because just as I was about to give up and backtrack, he did say there was a hole in the fence and that I could go through the hole and make it through Camp Pendleton. He also said that he would not admit he said that and that I was responsible for myself if anything happened. This solution was music to my ears, and I thanked him and was off. I did not know where I was going, but forward was better than backtracking in my book. It seemed to be my lucky day because a couple of guys on carbon fiber bikes, one from California and the other from Texas, said they overheard me talking with the ranger and that they knew of the hole in the fence shortcut. They said they would gladly show me.

I biked and conversed with great enthusiasm with my guides. The riding was smooth, on a deserted paved road, and when we got to the hole, it was no problem to bike through it. No one confronted us at any time. When the road ended, and the guides I was with were going a different way to get to their car, but they showed me the directions to get back on I-5.

I left the two guys and biked further down the deserted paved road. I had to take a right, bike under I-5, and then take the next sharp left onto the I-5 on-ramp. All was going to plan when suddenly, as I took the sharp left, I biked by three Marines on my right in full combat gear on military maneuvers as if in a war game. They were running by me to get to one of the five-ton military vehicles. One was carrying a standard issued M-16, another an M-60 machine gun, and a third had strapped to their back what appeared to be a bazooka. I could tell it was not live fire because one of the Marines had the red safety nozzle on their rifle. I must say I was not sure who was more surprised, the three Marines or myself. We were not worse for the encounter as they went on their way, and I boogied up the on-ramp to I-5. I looked further to my right and saw, beyond the trees, all kinds of military vehicles. It appeared a military vehicle staging area for military maneuvers was on the side of I-5, the main highway in California. It was awesome to see and a pleasant surprise. Perhaps I wasn't supposed to be in the area. Oops!

Once I got on to I-5, it was your typical slow-moving, bumper-to-bumper traffic. It was the California crawl. All was good because I was not in a car and blasted down the breakdown lane for eight miles on my fully loaded touring bike before getting off an exit headed for Oceanside. I was riding faster than the traffic and admittedly felt great satisfaction doing it to the chagrin of the folks in their hot vehicles.

Once at Oceanside, it was mostly highway biking with a bike lane and beach views on my right until I was just north of La Jolla. A pretty big hill separated me from the city. With great effort, I got up the hill. At the top, it was flat for some time. I knew I needed to bike back down the hill and pass the famous Scripps Institute of Oceanography. I was biking along when I saw a big descent, so I went down the massive hill without checking my map. I was feeling good and thoroughly enjoying the speed. Unfortunately, I noticed a sign that signaled I could turn onto I-5. I thought to myself, how could this be? I-5 is inland, and I should be near La Jolla Cove. I started to have a sinking feeling I missed my turn to go by the Scripps Institute

of Oceanography. I could feel my frustration boiling up as I started coming to terms with the fact I had made a colossal error. Once I got to the bottom of the hill, and at the intersection of I-5, I decided to check my cell phone app map. It confirmed I went down the wrong street. To get back on track, I would need to bike back up the hill. I was so upset at myself. I did not have the energy to bike back up the massive hill. I was also shocked that it seemed unlikely that I was going to get to Mission Beach by 6 pm. I was fuming. However, I realized I needed to regroup and use all the negative energy I was creating to problem solve and get myself going in the right direction. I saw on my map app that a bike trail cut across the University of California at San Diego campus to La Jolla Cove. By taking the trail, I would not have to bike up the hill. I would get lost some more trying to find my way through the University of California San Diego campus, but at least the campus was pretty and I was saving time. After thirty stressful minutes, I was back on course and heading into the city of La Jolla.

La Jolla was disappointing. The roads were terrible for biking because of all the potholes, bumps, and loose rock. It was also crowded and confusing to bike through. I was so happy to get to Mission Beach finally, but there must have been an event going on in Mission Beach because it was even more crowded than La Jolla. It had a Spring Break atmosphere. There were lots of cars, loud stereos, drunk people, and overall congestion. My past recollection of Mission Beach was so favorable and now it seemed like a crazy zoo that I wanted to escape as soon as possible. I was hoping to do a quick wheel dipping ceremony and leave. However, the beach was so crowded that I decided to bike to the far end of the beach. I then carried my bike to the edge of the tide line with my bike shoes on. It surprised me that I had a hard time finding a competent person to take a decent photo of me dipping my rear wheel in the Pacific Ocean. Either the picture was too close or too far, and one person couldn't figure out how to take a picture with my phone (yikes!). I then got strategic and found a teenager to help. Ultimately, the 14-year-old I asked took a great photo on his first try. Thank you, Generation Z.

    I got my picture with just enough light, but it was getting dark, and I still had no idea where I was going to be sleeping. Unfortunately, I got sand all over my shoes and bike. I needed to take time to take off as much sand as possible, as it could do damage to my bike components. The area seemed to be getting more and more crowded, and the number of cars and craziness was rising fast. As much as I was excited to get to La Jolla and Mission Beach, once I got there, I couldn't wait to leave because of the noise and crowds. I decided to bike to a Motel 6, which was about 4 miles away. The Motel 6 wasn't the best motel, but it was my only economical choice, and it was just off the Southern Tier bike path. Even with a military discount, it still cost me $81. I felt a little uncomfortable with the clientele, so I quickly got to my room and locked the door. I got to take a nice shower and put together my game plan for the next day. I was done with the Pacific Coast Bicycle Route and was in a position to take on the Southern Tier Bicycle Route.

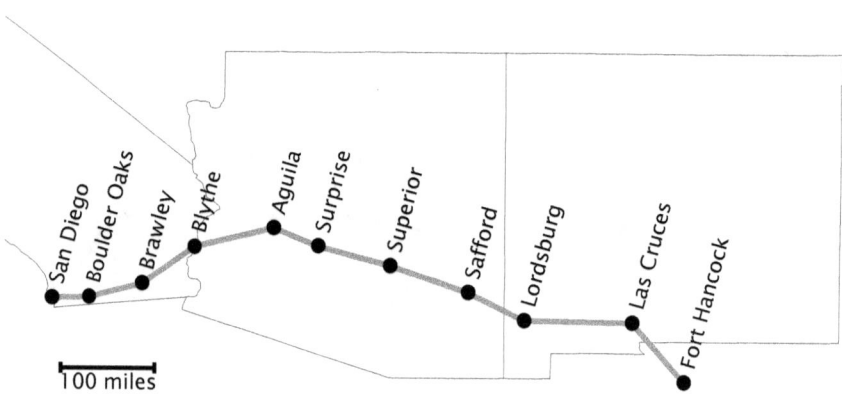

## Chapter 5: The Southern Tier Bicycle Route Begins – Challenge, Desert, People Power

*Day 8 – (60 miles) San Diego to Boulder Oaks Campground*

> *"Live life like you're the hero of your own movie."*
> *– Joe Rogan*

Tremendous anticipation came over me as I knew I was making a big decision to start a journey that was going to be among the most challenging adventures of my life. Biking down the west coast of the US was a piece of cake compared to biking across the country. At least on the west coast, I had the Pacific Ocean and all its artifacts to look at while I biked hundreds of miles in bliss; but heading east had deserts, remoteness, and potential danger. No wonderful vistas. Only what I perceived as a grind to the Atlantic Ocean; however, I did look forward to surprising my friend at his office in Valdosta, Georgia.

The first day of the Southern Tier is said to be the toughest. Many people quit on the first day because of the challenges. The biggest challenge involved biking from sea level to 4,200 feet in ninety-degree heat, with sparse desert becoming more prevalent with the increasing elevation and distance from San Diego.

Whatever fear or trepidation I might have been feeling needed to take a backseat to pure action. I tricked my psyche into believing it was just another day in paradise and that I needed my A-game to have a successful first day on the Southern Tier. If I had to climb Mount Everest on my bike, so be it. I would do it with vigor and not stop until I reached my planned destination 60 miles away.

The first few miles would be on bike paths, and I was surprised that the bike paths were older and didn't provide a smooth ride. My standards must be getting higher from all the bike paths that I had been on earlier. However, I was grateful that San Diego had bike paths because they certainly helped get me through a busy city that bustled with lots of cars and trucks.

According to my ACA bike map app, I had a steady incline all morning to Alpine, California. The map was correct. While the slope was real, I decided to take my time and not stress myself. It turned out the ride was pleasurable, and my tactic of at least telling myself I was going to take my time and not stress, seemed to be working. I just left my bike in granny gear and went with the flow. I was on a service road next to the highway, so there were few cars.

When I finally crested the massive hill into Alpine, I noticed on my map app that McDonalds was at the eastern end of town and not the closer west end. I had been visualizing this McDonalds on the hill all morning as if it was the Taj Mahal. In my "hangry" state, I thought there were some conspiracy and another example of the two-mile syndrome that the McDonalds was so far east. It didn't help that the temperature was 90 degrees. My misery index was quite high. Seeing that I am from the Northwest, we don't have a lot of heat, so I tend to start melting at 75 degrees.

The McDonalds in Alpine was quite lovely and a fitting sanctuary. It was air-conditioned and had plenty of fatty food and cold Coca-Cola, which my body was craving. I ate two lunches. I started getting so relaxed that I even started thinking of forgoing my goal of getting to Boulder Oaks Campground and camp in Alpine. I had read that the Alpine library had free camping. However, the more I thought about it, the more I felt that I was copping out. If I stopped in Alpine, which would be the easy thing to do, I would be setting a dangerous precedent so early in my mentally-challenging journey across the US. I then asked myself, "What would David Goggins do?" the media proclaimed the "toughest man in America" and over-all badass. He would remind me that "success is on the other side of suffering." He would then tell me to get my lazy ass back out in the hot weather, suck it up, and start biking east until I reach my destination. My inner Goggins voice was correct. I was going to make Boulder Oaks Campground if I had to crawl there. So, I jumped back on my bike in the overwhelming heat and slowly biked the last 25 miserable miles.

It was hot. There still seemed to be more unrelenting hills, and now I was biking on the highway with the added stress of cars and trucks blasting by me at 70 mph. It seemed so weird that one second, I could have all kinds of strength biking along, and then all of a sudden, my legs felt like two cast iron stove pipes incapable of generating any power to provide forward momentum. I ended up having to take a lot of water breaks and try to stretch out my legs. I was not going to quit, and having the goal of Boulder Oaks Campground helped focus me and push me forward. I quickly could have backtracked to Alpine and rested, but that was a no go in my book. It was Boulder Oaks or bust.

While taking a break at the first convenience store I'd seen since Alpine, I saw my first fellow cross-country bike tourist, who was from England. He was biking from the East Coast to San Diego. He was in a much better mood than I because he knew he only had one more incline before reaching Alpine, and then it was all downhill to the Pacific Ocean. He was excited to finish. I, on the other hand, had more hills, the scary desert, never-ending Texas, and about three thousand miles to go, so my enthusiasm was cautiously optimistic at best in the face of unknown adversity. We talked briefly, shared notes, and went our separate ways.

After lots of physical and mental effort, I finally made it to the Boulder Oaks Campground. It was only a 60-mile day, but it felt like a hundred-mile day. I was super excited to stop. I immediately found a campsite, cooked dinner, set up my tent, and eyed the toilets because I needed to go bad. I had been on the road for eight days, and I felt my body was not keeping up. I think my body, in general, was in shock from my relatively relaxed life at home to biking eighty miles a day, eating like a horse, and sleeping in a tent.

One thing I was pleasantly surprised at was that there were a lot of Pacific Crest Trail (PCT) hikers in camp. The campground represented the 25-mile mark of the PCT. The PCT was a very popular hiking trail from the border with Mexico to the border of Canada. It was a 2,650-mile hike and less than half who start it finish. I would meet many PCT hikers in the camp who just started their challenging journey. Since the tent sites were huge, one of the PCT hikers invited me to camp in his section. It was a nice gesture, but I told him I already had a tent site. However, not an hour later, as the sun was going down, a strange shadowy figure in what looked like a robe with a hood entered camp with no bike or backpack. He moved slowly and mysteriously towards the bathrooms. I wasn't sure the figure had legs. I was mesmerized by what I was seeing. My imagination started to take off as the citing reminded me of the scene in "The Resurrection of the Christ," where Mel Gibson is being crucified, looks out into the audience, and sees a hooded devil looking at him menacingly in his vulnerable state. Wow! I need to stop watching movies.

I was very suspicious of the stranger and had a bad feeling about him. All of a sudden, the PCT hiker's friendly gestures of having me camp in his site seemed like a great idea. After the shadowy figure moved to pass the road that separated me from the PCT hikers, I walked over to the PCT hikers to ask what they thought of the mysterious figure? They did not see the figure because they said, "What figure?" Yikes! I asked if I could move my tent to their site, and they said no problem. I am glad they didn't ask me why, or I would have had to admit I thought I saw the bogeyman.

### Day 9 – (94 miles) Boulder Oaks Campground to Brawley, California

> "Life begins at the end of your comfort zone."
> – Neale Donald Walsh

I can be such a stupid-ass sometimes. I decided to put my phone alarm on at its top volume so I could wake up very early and get an early start. The next morning, I was so tired that once the alarm sounded, it took me two minutes to figure out how to shut off my alarm because of my delirious state. I must have awoken the whole campground. I was embarrassed at my stupidity.

It didn't help that it was exceptionally cold as I got out of my sleeping bag. It was a balmy 39 degrees. I didn't realize how cold deserts can get even though it was 90 degrees the afternoon earlier. Due to the cold, I put on all my warm clothes, including fleece, raincoat, rain pants, a warm hat, and full-fingered gloves. I still wasn't warm or awake.

As soon as I left the campground, I started to ascend another decent-sized hill. You would think I was biking up Mount Everest with all the hill-climbing, but it is an illusion because all the descending would take seconds or minutes, and all the ascending would take minutes or hours. It was a bit frustrating to feel like you are going uphill all the time. And since I was doing a lot of uphill, I was getting hot quick. I did get a bit of a reprieve as I biked into the border community of Jacumba, California. It was interesting to see the infamous border wall less than a hundred yards away. I must say I didn't see any undocumented immigrants or any activity whatsoever at the border. It seemed all quiet on the southern front.

Once I finally got to the top of the mountain pass, which seemed to have many false passes, it was a short-lived victory as now it was time for the actual scary part – descending four thousand feet through a twisty, winding road with lots of speeding trucks and fifty-mile wind gusts that would come out of nowhere. It was white-knuckle riding time. As much as I love to bomb down a hill, especially to make some good time, I will listen to my gut when I feel something is not safe, and this downhill was one of those times. While I let gravity do

its thing, I did slow down when needed and had my hands ready to squeeze the brakes in an instant. The instant I felt or heard the wind or was taking a big winding curve, I erred on the side of slowing down or even stopping when a massive crosswind would happen. A few times, I had to lean into the wind to keep my balance. It was such an unnatural move that it could only be considered dangerous. This descent could be so much fun if it weren't for the crosswind. I had read in a blog post that a touring bicyclist died on this stretch when a crosswind blew him in front of a speeding truck. The danger was real and I took it seriously. I was relieved once I saw the desert floor. The end of the downhill was a straight descent into the desert where I only saw low grass, tumbleweeds, and not much else. I could see dunes in the distance and what was likely the Salton Sea area.

I biked from one uncomfortable area (the big hill) into another painful area (the hot, desolate desert). In the desert, I started with a tailwind for a 20 mile stretch of straight, flat road. There weren't many cars, and there were lots of quiet time to myself. At one point, I took a break and needed to put a new round of fresh butt cream for my seat to help fight saddle sores. I usually did this in a bathroom; however, there were no bathrooms for miles. I decided since no cars were coming to take a water break. I found a sign to lean my bike on, and I pulled my bike shorts down to air out my seat area. I walked around my bike exposed, got out my cream, and applied as needed. It felt free, reasonable, and no one saw me. Mission accomplished!

I found that since I was out in the desert, and there were very few cars, the idea of finding a bush or tree to pee behind was a waste of time. I started to pee off my stationary bike without getting off my bike. The method worked great, and every so often, I peed on my front tire, but it would quickly evaporate. I would institute this peeing method for the rest of my trip because, with the amount of water I was drinking, I had to pee all the time. It just wasn't time efficient to find somewhere private to pee.

The miles in the desert seem to go by quickly until I had a headwind that increased the suck factor dramatically. I was also battling a different kind of FOMO (fear of missing out). In bike touring terms, it was the fear of missing my turn and adding miles to my journey. Again, why I didn't buy a cell phone holder for my bike was killing me, and I would need to stop my bike often to check to make sure I did not miss my turn, especially when out in a desert.

I realized my attitude was terrible as I started in the desert. I kept telling myself the desert was dreary, it reminded me of death, and I couldn't wait to get out of the desert. This attitude was a downer, and within 10 miles in the desert, I was concerned I would not make it. However, I realized, as Zig Ziglar would say, "I needed a check-up from the neck up." I needed to change my attitude fast, or the consequences would be dire. I started to look for the beauty in the desert. As I did this, I started noticing the beautiful mountains out past the Mexican border, I started seeing more flowery bushes, and even more rabbits and lizards. I felt myself feel stronger, the more I concentrated on the absolute beauty and not the boredom of the desert.

As I was practicing my positive attitude therapy in my desert situation, my positive energy attracted me to an oncoming tandem bike. One of the real joys of biking across America is running into other bike tourists doing the same thing you are doing. You have an instant rapport with them and always treat them as long-lost friends you never met. It was a Dutch couple on a German-made, bomb-proof bike that I later learned could be folded up and shipped as baggage on a plane. San Diego was their destination. They were wonderfully positive. They were also a host of excellent route information as I headed east as I was good route intelligence as they headed west. There were lots of jokes and good comradery. We both could have broken out some beers and drank the afternoon and evening away telling stories and laughing at the trials and tribulations of the adventure we were on; however, we both had miles to do so after a seemingly too quick twenty minutes of banter. We wished each other well and basked in our glow of making a new friend.

After biking seven miles of the shittiest farming road I would encounter on the whole trip, I made it to a small farming town called Seeley. The Dutch couple was right. They told me it was better to bike on the gravel on the side of the road than on the road itself. I thought it was an odd piece of advice when they gave it to me, but it turned out 100% correct. The road I just rode on had big and little potholes as if a B-52 had carpet-bombed it.

After taking a Gatorade break in Seeley, I experienced my first ridiculously strong tailwind that blew me the next ten miles nearly without pedaling to El Centro, where I would get lunch.

After lunch, I enjoyed four more miles of strong tailwinds until I took a sharp left turn north that turned the strong tailwinds into a strong crosswind for the next ten miles as I headed towards Brawley. While the wind was bothersome, the flat farmland made for easy biking on another service road that kept me off Highway 111. The real bitch came when I had to take another left after ten miles and bike west directly into the strong headwind for two and a half miles. That was no fun, and after biking more than ninety miles in the hot desert, the curse words began to flow. I finally hit my destination, the Desert Inn, a cheap motel I found off of a fellow traveler's blog. It turned out to be a fortuitous move because the owner of the motel loved bicyclists and gave me the biker's rate of $50. He also offered to launder my clothes for free. How awesome after a tough biking day! It also helped that there was a Subway across the street and a grocery store across from the Subway. The owner also told me a fellow southern tier biker was staying in room 11 and that I should say "hi." I thought this was a great idea.

After I showered, ate, and went grocery shopping, I then knocked on room 11. It would be the first of many meetings with Ed. He was taking time out of work to check off a bucket list item to bike across the United States. He was a couple of years younger than me and was from the Boston area, not far from where I grew up. Ed was initially biking fifty to sixty miles per day but could bike much further. After twenty minutes of banter, we wished each other well and hoped we would bump into each other in the future. We did not talk about biking together because I liked to start early and was looking at doing another ninety-plus mile day while Ed woke up later and was happy with a fifty-plus mile day. However, we would meet many times again throughout the US over the next 35 days.

### Day 10 – (94 miles) Brawley to Blythe, California

> *"The happiest people spend much time in the state of flow, the state in which people are so involved in an activity that nothing else seems to matter ..."*
> – Mihaly Csikszentmihalyi

Wow! It was beautiful out as I biked east down Main Street and was looking forward to another long day on my bike. Today would be extra challenging because most of the ride was on Highway 78, and there appeared to be only a couple of small towns where I could take a break.

I was enjoying another early morning ride when a police car flew by me with their lights on. It seemed odd because there were few cars on the road and it was so early. After biking another couple of miles, I saw ahead that a state trooper had closed the highway. Once I caught up to the blockade, I asked if it was alright for me to bike through it because I was biking across the US, and this was the only route I knew to get to Blythe. The trooper said that I could not go past the blockade and suggested a twenty-mile alternate route. I looked at him as if to remind him that I was on a bike and not in a car. I then asked how long it would be before the highway would open, and he said it could be several hours. He then explained to me that there was an unfortunate accident with fatalities and that the investigation of the incident would take a while. I didn't know what to do, but it was apparent the state trooper wasn't letting me through. So, I turned north at the intersection and was brainstorming my options. I could wait until they open the road, or I could backtrack to town and wait at the Dunkin Donuts I saw, but backtracking is never a good idea. Just as I was thinking of what to do, I saw a farmer's road a half-mile away. It paralleled the highway. It was a dirt road, but since it hadn't rained in a while, it was pretty packed, and it looked like only farm trucks used it. I made the executive decision that I was going to use it to bypass the accident and then jump back onto the highway. I ended up biking for five miles on the dirt farm road and felt pretty sure I had passed the accident.

Once I got back on Highway 78, I had the road to myself for 15 miles. The open road made for some great biking. There was little to no wind, the sun was shining, and the way was straight with some hills. I biked by the Imperial Sand Dunes Recreation Area and could see the Chocolate Mountains on the horizon. One of the towns I was counting on there being a Subway turned out to be a one-store town. The place is pretty desolate except for a few times a year when over 100,000 dune buggy enthusiasts descend on the area.

The miles seem to go fast, and my fear of desert biking appeared to be melting away. While it would have been nice to see a restaurant the first seventy miles of my bike ride, I had extra food and six liters of water on my bike. Later, I was told and didn't realize that Highway 78 was a dangerous road for bikers because of the hills, people driving fast, and there were no actual bike lanes. Ignorance must have been my bliss as I stayed as far right as I could, and other than large trucks blasting by me, I felt pretty safe. Once I hit Palo Verdi, I finally saw a little local grocery store and bought some snacks, the usual Cheetos and Gatorade, and relaxed in the shade outside the store. As I was relaxing, I all of a sudden saw Ed pull up on his bike. He surprised me because we were about seventy-five miles away from Brawley, and I thought he was taking his time. I was glad to see him. He said he left the motel at about 7 am then saw the roadblock, but the officer was busy talking to someone else, so he just biked through the barricade, and when the officer called out to him, he just gave a friendly wave as if he didn't realize he wasn't supposed to go forward. The state trooper did not give chase, and he biked past the accident. He said it was a horrific scene as the accident involved a truck and a car at an intersection. The truck was blocking the highway and had been on fire. The car was totaled. All the injured and killed had been taken away by the time he got there. He had to be careful with avoiding the glass from the crash, but he said everyone was cool with him passing by going northwest to Blythe. I thought it was pretty gutsy of Ed to do what he did, but I understood the idea of waiting or biking an alternate route was not appealing when you have mileage goals. Also, I think Ed had a revelation that there was no reason he couldn't do more than fifty or sixty miles a day as long as you start early enough. We talked for a while, and then he was off to continue ahead. Ed's goal was to reach the Arizona border that day.

As for myself, I had a Warmshower stay in Blythe, so I knew I only had twenty miles of flat farmland riding to go to reach it. It turned out to be great riding as there was a slight tailwind, and the miles were a blur. Once I got to Blythe, I stopped at a Hardees for a quick burger before I headed over to my Warmshower stay. I noticed my Warmshower host was three miles off the route, and I was looking to see if there was any camping nearby so I wouldn't have to go the extra miles. After doing some research, the Warmshower stay seemed like my best option.

At the Hardees, I met my second bike tourist biking west to east across the US. His name was Don, and he was from Long Beach, California. Don seemed like a likable guy and was excited about his trip. It is funny whenever I meet another biker, I think whether it would be a good idea to join forces so that we would have someone to enjoy the ride with across the US. Ed seemed like a natural, but he was doing his own thing, and I could respect that. So, I asked Don some questions, and the more I talked to him, the more I realized it was not a good fit to ride with Don. For one, Don was a little older, not as fit as I, and he was riding a modified mountain bike, which looked slower. He then told me some stories that made me question his judgment. He told me that he decided to bike from Long Beach directly over the mountains, and he tried to use Google maps to cross the Salton Sea.

The problem with Google maps is sometimes, especially in rural areas, the maps do not get updated, and unfortunately, Don followed a deserted road in the Salton Sea that turned into him walking his bike twelve miles in the sand before he realized he was in serious trouble. Recognizing his predicament, he was lucky he still had cell service, so he called the area sheriff to see if someone in a four-wheel-drive truck could rescue him. The sheriff laughed and said we have something even better. Within ten minutes, a Search and Rescue helicopter on a training run swooped by and rescued Don. As Don told me his story, I thought it sounded outrageous and like a tall tale until Don showed me video footage on his cell phone. I was amazed. I thought it made for a great story, but it wasn't sufficient to make me feel confident about biking with him across the US. The death knell was when I asked him where he was sleeping because I thought if he needed a place, I could call my super kind Warmshower hosts. He said he was going to camp out by the river. His rationale was, "if it was good for the homeless, it was good for him." Don was a man of God sponsored by a church group, so he had God on his side, looking over him during his journey. After eating my burger, I wished Don the best and headed to my Warmshower host. The irony is I would see Don again.

My Warmshower hosts operated out of a tackle shop that sold live tackle. My hosts were super hospitable and let me set up in the back of the store by their rather large goose who was territorial. My host warned me the goose might come up to my tent and squawk but not to pay too much attention. I set up my tent and gave the goose its space. One cool thing about my host site was that they had a little social area where I cooked and ate dinner, and the local farmers would stop by for a drink and some conversation. They were a lot of fun to talk to and shared stories of living as a farmer in the Imperial Valley. They had lots of questions regarding my bike trip and were in awe of the miles covered. Later they had loud music, and even more people showed up. I stayed in my tent in back surfing the internet on my phone and making phone calls. I also was making it a habit to post on Facebook once a day about my travels, so that family and friends knew what I was up to and knew that I was still alive.

## THE SOUTHERN TIER BICYCLE ROUTE BEGINS

### Day 11 – (90 miles) Blythe, California to Aguila, Arizona

> *"To be yourself in a world that is constantly trying to make you something else is the greatest accomplishment."*
> – Ralph Waldo Emerson

I woke up knowing I had a long desert stretch that seemed a bit intimidating. I acknowledged there was no use in wasting energy on irrational fear, and the only solution was to get on my bike and move forward. My fears were like annoying gnats. I just wanted to swat them away. While my confidence biking in the desert was strengthening, I still had moments of weakness because of the mystery that awaited my day.

It didn't take me long to hit the Arizona line. It was a significant landmark as I had one state down. I was making progress, and it only took me three days to cross California. Once in Arizona, I jumped on Interstate 10 and headed east. I heard some rumors that some cyclists stay on I-10 to just before Phoenix. It cuts out quite a bit of mileage. The day before, I had talked to Ed about the idea, and he said he was considering it. I gave myself until Quartzsite to decide whether I was going to head to Phoenix on I-10 or follow the established ACA route that took Highway 60 to Wickenburg, before taking Highway 60 south into Phoenix. It was longer but safer for a bicyclist. It was more scenic. I decided to have breakfast in Quartzsite as I saw they had a McDonalds. I was starting to recognize all the biking I was doing had already worked off any reserves I may have had, and I seemed to be hungry all the time. McDonalds was always a great stop because the food was cheap, consistent, and enjoyable. The facilities were clean, they had bathrooms that worked, and their WiFi was excellent. When you are trying to ride a lot of miles, consistency and speed was essential, and McDonalds never disappointed. It is funny: before the trip I hardly ate at McDonalds, but now that I was on the road, I realized Morgan Spurlock from the movie *Super-Size Me* had nothing on my McDonald eating habits.

As I left Quartzsite, I decided to bike up Highway 60 towards Wickenburg. My goal was Aguila, which was about twenty miles south of Wickenburg. Biking on Highway 60, I had a bothersome headwind most of the way. It was my first long, sustained headwind I had had for most of a day. Headwinds will drain you and make your biking less fun, especially when you have a goal to bike over ninety miles. If I didn't have a purpose, I would probably have a much shorter day, but then it would take me forever to get across the country. There was a part of me that realized that time was money. Each day I was biking was costing me money. Most people who think about biking across America or even hiking the Pacific Crest Trail or the Appalachian Trail first think of the physical challenge, but the second thing to think about is the financial cost of such an endeavor. Some people can travel on the cheap, $10 to $29/day, by wild camping and cooking all their meals, but that would be the minority. Most people eat fast food or in restaurants, camp or get a motel, have bike repairs, do laundry, need a shower, etc. Touring can add up. Someone crossing the US can look to spend from $30 to $100+ per day if they are self-supported. A supported trip across the US can easily cost between seven and ten thousand dollars.

I continued to struggle against the headwind as I plowed along on Highway 60. Unfortunately, I was a little late for the super wildflower bloom, but I did see some remnants which momentarily quenched my thirst for color out in the desert. The desert does have its beauty with subtle shades of various colors and lots of variety of cactuses; however, I am more of a mountain, glacier, turquoise lake kind of guy so the desert would slowly become an acquired taste.

After 9 hours on the bike, I finally made it to Aguila. Unfortunately, my Warmshower hosts were out of town, but they did tell me to go to the town library, and they would leave me a $15 food voucher and directions to free camping. I got to the library and walked in a sweaty mess. I asked if someone left me an envelope. I half expected the librarian to think I was crazy, but she understood what I was saying as if it happened all the time and gave me the envelope left by my hosts.

In the envelope was a kind note, a $15 food voucher for a local restaurant, and directions to free camping at the town park. It was a pleasant surprise. I was super appreciative of the kindness of my Warmshower hosts. Once I got the envelope, I decided to spend some time in the library as it was only 4 pm. I used their internet service to post on my Facebook page and catch up on the news of the day. Aguila, was one of the few places where my Cricket wireless did not work at all, but the library WiFi was free.

The $15 food voucher was a godsend. I went to a local eatery that looked like an absolute dive, and the waitress was very inattentive; however, I ordered real food in Steak and Eggs, and it was phenomenal. My body perked up after a real meal. Unfortunately, after sitting for an hour in the restaurant, the lactic acid invaded my body, and I was moving at the speed of molasses. I had some severe old-man-itis going on, but I forced myself on my bike and biked over to the town park. It seemed odd to be camping in the town park, but they had grills, and it looked like others had done it in the past. At the moment, I was the only one in the park with the intention of camping. Before setting up the tent, I decided to again bike back into town to use the free WiFi at the library.

As it was getting dark, I headed back to the town park to set up my tent when I was happy to see Ed. I could tell he had a rough day. He also was a victim of the harsh headwind conditions. I could empathize with Ed. He did not participate in Warmshowers, so he needed to go into town and get some food. I watched his gear as I was setting my tent up. We then shared some food and some beer he bought me for my birthday that was the next day.

The only downer about camping in the town park was that there were no shower facilities. I would take a wet wipes bath. It seemed to clean me a little, but once I went to bed, I slept in my sweaty funk. It was uncomfortable and not conducive to a sound sleep.

### Day 12/13 – (59 miles/zero-day) Aguila to Surprise, Arizona

*"There are no strangers here; only friends you haven't met yet."*
*– William Butler Yeats*

I was up early, and there was no stirring in Ed's tent, so I tried to be as quiet as possible so as not to wake him. I was off in the crisp morning air. I loved the freedom of the road a bike trip can give you. I seemed to be much stronger on the saddle because I had a great, high caloric meal for dinner. One massive benefit of starting early in the morning is that the winds are negligible until about 9:30 am, so it was a good time to do some serious mileage before the wind could be a factor. This morning I was biking with purpose as I knew there was a McDonalds in Wickenburg about twenty-five miles away. After breakfast, I would be visiting a friend's mom, who agreed to host me in Surprise, Arizona.

I seemed to be getting more comfortable with my morning biking routine because my irrational fears seemed to subside, and the confidence of getting up and getting her done was taking over. I knew I had miles to complete, and I would do them. It was always a benefit if there were some beautiful mountains, fields of wildflowers, or some wildlife running across the road to distract me from the sameness of biking big miles every day. My imagination was always on overdrive but I mostly spent my biking hours thinking of logistics like where am I going to eat, sleep, who am I going to meet, where should I stop today, should I camp or stay at a motel, what am I going to post on my Facebook page today, and on and on.

My McDonalds stop consisted of the usual big breakfast with hotcakes (1350 calories) and a medium coffee with one cream. I also made it a routine to first stop in the bathroom to take off my bike shorts and put on loose shorts to let me seat area dry out. I would also put my bike shorts out nasty, sweaty side up in the sun so that they would dry up. While my saddle sores were getting better, they were still an issue I needed to be diligent about as I continued my ride. Good hygiene was critical. Once I finished my breakfast, I would go back in the bathroom, put a new round of butt cream or bug balm on and then put my dry bike shorts back on. This system, along with "mashing" every five to ten minutes on my bike seemed to be helping with the saddle sores.

It was only about thirty-four miles to Surprise. I felt great as I was flying down the highway at greater than 15 mph, and I looked forward to meeting my friend's mom and having a unique experience staying in a retirement community. I had texted my friend's mom that I would arrive later in the afternoon, but I had been biking so well that I had done 59 miles before the noon hour, and I had to text her again to see if I could get there earlier. She said no problem.

I was excited to meet my friend's mom, but it was a bit awkward only because we had never met. Once I arrived, my friend's mom, whose name was Carol, was amiable and hospitable. Once Carol showed me my room, I immediately took off my sweaty, stinky clothes, put my clothes in the wash, and then took a shower. Within 45 minutes, I was like a new person in a charming home, relaxed. Carol showed me around her house, and I met her brother, who just came to live with Carol from Central America. Carol was a world traveler and had lots of great stories to share, including stories about her daughter, who I knew from my local Toastmasters club. After hanging with Carol for a few hours, I went shopping in the shopping district just outside the retirement community. The retirement community itself was beautiful with manicured lawns, bike lanes, and even a golf course. All the houses were the same color, and it was just immaculate and well kept. It was a relaxing place.

I planned to get my groceries and supplies needed for the next few days as I planned on heading out the following day into the desert.

I did not know the next time I would hit a decent grocery store. I also took the opportunity to review my gear to make sure everything was in working order and to repair any items that needed fixing. Two things required repair: my helmet and my bike shoes. My helmet's visor would rise with headwind and be useless. I needed to get the visor to stay in place. After some deliberation, I realized I had one zip tie left, so I decided to use it to hold the visor in place. It worked like a charm and ended up lasting the rest of the ride. My other gear needing repair was my darn bike shoe that was starting to separate in two. I tried to look around for some decent bike shoes, and I saw that REI Phoenix was too far away, so I decided to use more duct tape to put three binds (front, middle, and back of the shoe) to hold the shoe together. Carol gave me some black duct tape, which made my shoe look a little better than the tacky gray tape.

Since April 5th was my birthday, Carol took me, her brother, and a friend out for dinner at the local community restaurant. It was a remarkable gesture that surprised me. It was a great time, and made my stay even more special. I am humbled by how kind people had been treating me on the trip and grateful for any hospitality I received.

The next morning, I woke up early, and Carol was up and made some fantastic coffee. It certainly tasted good, but I had loaded up my bike, put my bike clothes on, and fully intended to leave right at 6 am. However, as happened when I hung out with Keith in San Luis Obispo, I was offered a second cup of coffee. I couldn't refuse. I felt so relaxed with great company and good coffee that I ended up staying with Carol for a second day. It just made such sense since I hadn't taken a zero-day yet and had biked over a thousand miles in 12 days. It would also give my saddle sores the time to heal and my body the time to rejuvenate.

With my zero-day, I walked around the retirement community, ate a lot of food at Chipotles, In-and-Out Burger, and Chick-fil-A, hung out on the side of Carol's pool, and made it a point not to ride my bike. My zero-day was a success. What made my second day stay even better was I had the opportunity to go to a big community party that night at one of Carol's friend's house. I found that those older adults know how to party. It was an amicable, fun atmosphere in the retirement community. I felt I could get used to living here. I even met one couple who were so fascinated with my trip that they called a friend in Silver City, New Mexico while at the party with a few drinks in us to see if she would host me in a few days when I was biking

through the area. It seemed unusual. I think it caught their friend by surprise. When the couple handed me the phone to talk to her friend, it seemed a bit awkward, but I decided to roll with it. She asked me questions like "Am I a serial killer?" which I found hilarious, but I asked her if she was Kathy Bates from the movie *Misery*? *Misery* was a movie where Kathy Bates abducts a man, James Caan, ties him to a bed, and breaks his ankles so he can't leave her. She laughed and agreed to host me when I was in the area. I told her I was not sure when I would be there because I never know about the weather, whether my bike would breakdown or whether I would break down, so I said I would contact her one or two days before I was in her area. After the party I went home and slept in the most comfortable bed I would for many days.

### Day 14 – (94 miles) Surprise to Superior, Arizona

> *"One travels to run away from routine, that dreadful routine that kills all imagination and all our capacity for enthusiasm."*
> – Ella Maillart

I was determined to leave again at 6 am and was not going to succumb to "Second Cup of Coffee Syndrome" – the agreeing to the second cup of coffee, even when I know better that causes me to lose focus and take more time off the bike. While I was very focused on completing my daily mileage and getting closer to my ultimate goal, I also knew it was easy to get seduced into relaxing. I found it helpful to have a goal to start the day and to stick to it. If my goal was to leave at 6 am, then I would go at 6 am. That is what I did. It was hard to leave the comfortable confines of Carol's home and her excellent hospitality; however, I had mileage to make as I knew it wasn't going to make itself.

After leaving the retirement community, I would cut through the Phoenix area in local neighborhoods with well-manicured green lawns (it was still April) and bike paths that ran through the city. I pretty much stuck to a beautiful trail along an aqueduct that took me to Arizona State University in Tempe.

After lunch, I had a huge decision to make. The decision was whether I was going to follow the ACA preferred safe route that headed north into the Tonto National Forest and then south towards Globe, Arizona, or to take the highway towards Superior that would take me through a dangerous quarter-mile tunnel with no bike lanes. I read many blogs that mentioned about the hazardous tunnel and lack of bike lanes while speeding trucks let you know how insignificant you were in the hierarchy of moving vehicles. Ed and I talked about this decision a few days ago when we were in Aguila, and we both seemed to lean towards going the tunnel route.

I did not decide which route I was not going to take until I got to the point of no return where I needed to either make a left to go north or straight to go towards the tunnel. I realized the long way added 61 miles and eleven thousand feet of elevation gain through roads that had sections with no bike lanes, and the shortcut shortened the trip by 61 miles but was deemed unsafe. I decided since I took a zero-day and didn't see anything in the long way that intrigued me, taking the shortcut was the best option for me. I also planned to bike to just before the tunnel and find a place to sleep so I could tackle the tunnel first thing in the morning. I figured that the traffic and, more specifically, the truck traffic would be less at 6 am.

The ride to Superior was up some decent elevation but on a broad highway with excellent bike lanes. The thought that this road was dangerous was not correct. I had read that the highway department was taking measures to make the highway safer for bicyclists and thought they did a great job. I didn't find any part of the road to Superior dangerous in any way. I thought everyone must be crazy. Even Ed sent me a text warning me not to take the tunnel because he found it was dangerous. He was emphatic that the ride to Globe, through the tunnel area, was the most miserable experience he had since being on the Southern Tier. I didn't understand his message with my current knowledge of the road; however, the next day, I would!!

Once I got to Superior after a long day of biking through the hot desert, I had no idea where I was going to be staying for the evening. I did not want to get a motel and was keen on camping. However, I decided to check my Warmshower app to see if there were any hosts in the area. It just so happened that there was one. I decided to give them a call, which is usually against acceptable protocol as it is kinder to ask with a three-day notice. I called the hosts, and they were super friendly but said they already were hosting a couple in their RV in their back yard that night. I then asked if there was any camping in the area. After some silence, the host all of a sudden asked me if I wasn't concerned with having water in my place, that they had a mini-RV I could stay in for the night. I was okay with the arrangement. They gave me the address, and I went to their home.

The first thing I noticed was there were a lot of dogs barking in the neighborhood. My host showed me the cute mini-RV. It looked great to me. There was no shower, and the bathroom was at the convenience store down the street. It was not the ideal set up, but it was available and free. It would certainly suit my needs. I felt I could suck it up for a day, especially after having two wonderful relaxing days at Carol's sanctuary in Surprise.

The mini-RV ended up being awesome. I did ask my Warmshower host about the tunnel and the road ahead, and he seemed to think it was safe. Boy! I have to say I disagreed with him once I completed it the next day.

### Day 15 – (110 miles) Superior to Safford, Arizona

*"The real voyage of discovery consists of not seeing new landscapes but in having new eyes."*
*– Marcel Proust*

As I left Superior, I was a little fearful but up for the challenge before me. I felt comforted by the words of my Warmshower host; however, I also contemplated the conflicting text from Ed saying it was the worst part of the ride, and he would advise me not to bike the shortcut. At this point, I was committed at 6 am and headed for the tunnel.

The highway to the tunnel was a steady incline. There seemed to be more cars and trucks than I thought there would be at this time of the morning. While I had fear about the tunnel, I noticed I was developing more confidence in myself overcome challenges I was meeting on the bike trip.

I was already sweating bullets as I saw the entrance to the tunnel ahead. I stopped just before the tunnel to determine whether it was better to walk the bike on the small walk path or to gut it out and go for it on the road. I looked back to see if any trucks were coming and said, "screw it" and started biking slightly uphill through the tunnel on the road. There was no bike lane and very little room on the right. Cars were passing me, and within the tunnel, they sounded like

trucks. I was biking in my granny gear as far right as I could, pedaling as fast as I could and was gritting my teeth, thinking I can't wait to get out of this tunnel. I had no rear mirror to see what was behind me and just had to rely on the drivers behind me seeing my flashing red light attached to my rear left pannier. Most cars passed me on the far lane, but even then, the vehicles sounded so loud because of the echoes in the tunnel. It was nerve-racking, but I concentrated on moving forward in a steady, straight manner. I was 100% focused and doing my absolute best to relax within all the crazy noise from the cars and trucks going both directions. When I finally got through the quarter-mile tunnel, I was very relieved, but I still had another hundred yards to get to a pullout. I then noticed once out of the tunnel there was no bike or break down lane going forward.

Just as I got to the pullout, I looked back, and the biggest 18-wheeler truck I had ever seen blasted through the tunnel in the far-right lane I was in and flew past me within six feet of my bike. The wind produced almost blew me over. The sound and size of the truck freaked me out and would have traumatized me in the tunnel. I felt so fortunate not to have been in the tunnel with that particular truck.

After I took a quick water break and regrouped, I continued on the highway toward Globe. I was starting to realize what Ed was saying about the road being so scary. No bike lane and vehicles were flying by me at 70 mph. After about thirty minutes of biking on the highway, my psyche had enough. I decided the stress was too much, and it simply was not safe, so I decided to take an extended "walking break." I walked on the right side of my bike, keeping my bike between me and the traffic. I probably walked like this for a couple of miles until the road opened up a bit and started going downhill.

After a while, I couldn't wait to get to Globe, still 15 miles away. So, I decided to trust my biking skills and biked as fast as I could, going with the traffic as far right as possible. I knew there was a McDonalds in Globe, and I could use a heavy fat meal. After I biked past the mine, the traffic became less of a burden, but my resolve to get to McDonalds did not waver.

After completing my saddle-sore routine and eating another big breakfast, I was determined to make more mileage because I just got another text message from a Warmshower host that I could stay in Safford, Arizona. The only problem was that it would end up a 105-mile day for me to get to Safford from where I started. The first twenty-five miles were very stressful. I needed the last eighty to be a lot easier.

I left McDonalds like a bullet and was determined to make some serious mileage. I had picked out a couple of landmarks to make sure I hit to assure me I was going in the right direction. It is funny because I always have a fear of going the wrong way and adding miles. I was determined not to make such a stupid mistake.

After biking for fifteen minutes, I started to realize that I did not see my landmarks yet. I was surprised I was not out of the main section of the town. Evil thoughts began creeping into my head that I might be going the wrong direction, but I thought that was impossible because I was diligent not to make such a stupid mistake. However, after twenty minutes, I was still in a busy section of town and did not pass my landmarks. I was checking my map app, but everything seemed the same, and I couldn't exactly tell where I was. I was still in denial that I could be going the wrong direction. I then asked a guy coming out of a gas station which way it was to Safford. He confirmed I was going the wrong way. Ughh! I was so mad at myself. I had just biked two and a half miles downhill in the wrong direction after I just gave myself an internal lecture on the reasons not to go the wrong route. At this point, I was dropping copious f-bombs to myself as I start biking up the hill towards McDonalds. I was fuming. I tried to direct the energy into my pedals as I berated myself for my stupidity. I could think that most McDonalds I seem to hit always appear to be on the opposite side of the road, so I tend to bike across the street and start heading east/southeast; however, this time I was already on the right side of the road but simply needed to take a right out the McDonalds to continue southeast, but something in me made me cross the street. It proves I am such a creature of habit. Stupid! Stupid! Stupid!! I was seething. I certainly hope no one was filming me because I was having a total emotional intelligence breakdown and would undoubtedly be embarrassed at my behavior. As I passed the McDonalds, I got even madder because I just made what seemed like an impossibly long day of 105 miles, now 110 miles. I was also heading up another hill, which made things even worse. The only good coming from this moment was that I was so mad that I started biking as fast as I could using all my negative energy. However, after ten miles, I realized that I still was super pissed off and that if I continued the way I was going, I would burn out, so I saw a gas station on the left side of the highway. I decided to stop for a Gatorade break.

I walked into the gas station, trying not to show how pissed I was and not displace my anger in any way. I paid for my large Gatorade, walked outside, and just tried to relax by myself out on the sidewalk with my bike in the shade. Just as I was trying to reach some equilibrium, an Indian man, perhaps an Apache as I was in Apache country, started asking me about my bike ride. I was polite and was trying my best to answer his questions, but I also realized I needed some serious time to myself because I was so upset at my stupidity. I think the guy sensed I wasn't all there and wished me well as he jumped in his car. I felt kind of bad because I would have loved to talk to him further, but at the same time, I realized I needed to recover from my meltdown. Ironically, the guy asking me questions did help me get out of my funk because I genuinely appreciated him asking questions and being interested in my trip. It was at that point that a light bulb came on, and I realized my trip was more than just biking miles and seeing the scenery of the south. It was also about meeting the people of the south and learning from them.

After fifteen minutes, I was back on the road in a better place mentally. The way was pretty much flat with some long slow uphill and downhill sections. I must have reached the flow state as I biked down Highway 60 towards Safford because the miles just added up, and before I knew it, I hit a little Indian town of Bylas, with several gas stations. Sure enough, I had another Gatorade break, and another Apache man started to talk to me about my bike trip. I loved the guy's energy and interest. I was in a much better place mentally to speak to this guy than the guy at my last rest break. I realized all the time on my bike by myself was nice, but I appreciated some interpersonal communication. I seemed to receive it during breaks from strangers asking questions about biking or my bike trip.

I finally made it to Safford and ate dinner at a Subway before I called Hal, my Warmshower host. Luckily, Hal only lived one mile from the Subway, and I quickly biked over to his apartment. It was great to meet Hal as he was an old retired college professor who hosted up to 60 bicyclists a year through Warmshowers. Hal was a gregarious man and was super hospitable. He showed me around his place, showed me where I would sleep on a blowup mattress on the floor, and he made me a fruit bowl. The fruit was much needed as I had just biked my longest day yet of 110 miles. My day started rough but ended with determination to reach my goal of Safford. I was happy with myself, and I was delighted to be talking to Hal as he was a great adventurer himself and had all kinds of interesting stories to share. He was also an Apache history enthusiast who knew of the rich history of this section of Arizona. It is funny; I had told Hal that I was debating which Warmshower host to contact as there were two in Safford. He said they both were great friends, but he said while both are great hosts, one you sleep in a barn on a massage table and the other, with Hal, you sleep in the living room on an inflatable mattress. I think I got the better deal.

### Day 16 – (76 miles) Safford, Arizona to Lordsburg, New Mexico

*"And there is the most dangerous risk of all, the risks of spending your life not doing what you want on the bet you can buy yourself the freedom to do it later."*
*– Randy Komisar*

I stayed for only one cup of coffee with Hal. Hal did offer me a second cup and to stay an extra day, but I told him "the road is calling, and I must go."

It was a flat ride with little wind to New Mexico. The first sixty-five miles were a blissful blur. It was hot as it hit ninety degrees, and I realized my thick eyebrows were being a problem as they were retaining a lot of water. The water would drip on my glasses to the point I couldn't see out of them. My Portuguese eyebrows were officially a problem and I would have to wipe the dripping water from my sunglasses continually. It was indeed a first world problem.

I could feel I was getting stronger on the bike and started thinking of biking to Silver City, but that would entail a 130-mile day, and that would be overdoing it. As I got into New Mexico, the wind started picking up, but it was good it was a westerly wind, so it was a tailwind. As I got closer to Lordsburg, the wind got stronger, and I realized any direction other than biking east, the wind was going to be a problem.

I had received a text message from Ed asking where I was and where I was stopping. We agreed to meet somewhere in Lordsburg for a late lunch. Once I took a right turn off Highway 70 to get to downtown Lordsburg, the wind started to be a big problem. The crosswind/headwind was unrelenting and made biking miserable. It didn't help that Lordsburg was an odd town to ride a bike in because the streets were going weird directions because of how the highway cut the city in half. I stopped at the Chamber of Commerce to get some information about the town because I could see nowhere to eat. The town was beaten down and depressed. It was too windy to continue to Silver City. I was ready to call it a day at 2 pm.

As I was in the chamber, I saw Ed pull up to my bike. It is easy to find a fellow biker in a town. Look for their fully-loaded bike in front of an establishment. I told Ed there was a McDonalds up ahead, so we went there to discuss our next move. We both ordered some food and immediately checked the forecast on our phones. The wind was supposed to get worse into the afternoon and be even worse the next day. The wind was forecast to blow a steady twenty-eight plus miles per hour with gusts of more than 60, mostly coming from the west.

The forecast was terrible news as both Ed and I were planning on heading north to Silver City. Ed and I brainstormed while eating our McDonalds. We realized we had a problem as biking into a thirty to sixty mph crosswind was a recipe for misery and danger. Also, the weather would be freezing, and it could snow in the mountains over the next two or three days. We were stuck and didn't want to take a zero-day in a sleepy town like Lordsburg that didn't even have a bar, although they did have a McDonalds. We realized we had three choices: a zero-day, a miserable, dangerous day heading north to Silver City, or to use our situation, strong westerly winds, to our advantage. We decided to sleep on it and decide in the morning after checking the latest forecast.

Once we came up with a loose plan for the next day, we needed a place to camp. However, the wind was so strong it would be difficult to set up and stay in a tent, so we joined forces and split the fee for a cabin at the local KOA. It was the first time I could get a discount for being a veteran, and I would find out it would not be the last.

After setting up at the KOA, Ed and I ate dinner at a local restaurant with another eastbound biker to discuss our plans for the next day. As we received our food, I looked out the window and couldn't believe my eyes when I saw Don (who I met in Blythe) biking up the road. He looked tired and worried. I tried to get his attention in the restaurant, but he was too busy and focused looking for a place to stay. I wanted to run out to see him, but the waitress was serving our food. I saw him biking into a local motel, and that would be last I would see of Don. I have to say I was amazed to have seen Don this far from where we last spoke in Blythe. I speculated he must have stayed on I-10 through Phoenix, so he made excellent time to make it to Lordsburg.

### Day 17 – (120 miles) Lordsburg to Las Cruces, New Mexico

> *"Life should not be a journey to the grave with the intention of arriving safely in a pretty and well-preserved body, but rather to skid in broadside in a cloud of smoke, thoroughly used up, totally worn out, and loudly proclaiming 'Wow! What a ride!'"*
> – Hunter S. Thompson

Ed and I woke up early and checked the forecast. The forecast remained the same as predicted. After a short discussion, we decided our best option was to use the wind to our advantage and head east to Las Cruces on Highway I-10. Wow! We were in for an exciting journey.

It was 6:30 am, and the wind was 15 mph coming from the west. Ed and I decided it was best to bike together for safety, and we had the same goal of making it 120 miles to Las Cruces by the end of the day. As we got onto I-10, I was feeling strong on the bike. Ed was in front because he had a mirror so he could see behind him. We had a vast breakdown lane to bike in; however, for some odd reason, it oscillated between a clean road and a very bumpy, dirty pathway with all kinds of rocks and foreign objects on the road that could puncture your tire.

Ed and I biked together for about fifteen miles when all of a sudden, I saw Ed's back wheel blow up. Neither he nor I knew what he hit, but it did result in a flat. We both stopped and then noticed how strong the tailwind was as it was blowing over thirty mph. It was hard to fix Ed's tire as the wind was blowing the bike and repair kit supplies all over the place. Ed was surprised I stuck around, but I felt we were in it together, so I helped out where I could as Ed fixed his tire. After about twenty-five minutes, we were back on the road, and we recognized the benefit of the mighty wind. According to Ed's computer, we started averaging over 23 miles per hour, which meant we were going by mile markers every two-plus minutes, which made the miles fly by fast. We got to Deming, which was the halfway point at sixty miles, a little past 10 am, which was unreal. The wind was blowing us real hard, but I barely felt it. It was like I was having a good biking day, and when there was a big wind gust, it felt like a soft nudge in the right direction. The wind was blowing the perfect direction, although we also had a weird periodic crosswind that would blow tumbleweeds, which some had thorns, into our bikes as we were riding east. We even biked through some developing dust storms, which can be extremely dangerous as they could reduce the visibility on a highway.

Once we got to Deming, the wind was blowing about thirty-five mph and was dangerous if you were not riding in an easterly direction. We went to the local McDonalds for a quick meal, and some of the patrons were warning us how dangerous it was to be out riding a bike. They were so concerned they offered us to let us stay at their house and called us crazy for even considering biking with the winds so strong. While I took their concerns seriously, Ed was adamant that because we were going east that we were safe. We thanked the patrons for their concerns, but we were back on the road as the winds got even stronger. It was hard to bike north onto the onramp because the wind was blowing so hard; however, once we were heading up the ramp going due east, the wind blew into our backs, and we flew up the ramp like a rocket.

It seemed like the wind was getting even stronger once we got out of McDonalds, and a severe dust storm was taking place that blackened the sky and reduced visibility. I have to admit I was getting a bit concerned because I realized that looking at a map, there was nothing in the sixty miles between where we were in Deming and Las Cruces. So, if we had a situation, whether we blew a tire or had some serious mechanical issue, we were screwed with no way out except to beg for a ride on the highway. As we got back on the highway, the dust storm was raging, and you could barely see down the highway. Another danger we recognized was a state trooper driving up and down the highway determining whether it was too dangerous to be driving on the highway in a car or truck, never mind a bicycle. That would be another issue: if they closed the highway, where would we go. It is probably not surprising to say that Ed and I were the only bicyclists on the highway at that time. The other Southern Tier bicyclist we had dinner with the night before decided to stay in Deming to wait out the storm.

Within two miles of leaving Deming, Ed blew his back tire again. He had two thorns or screws embedded in his rear tire. It looked terrible; however, Ed pulled the objects out, and because he had self-sealing tires, he put more air in the tires, and the sealant plugged the holes, so this tire repair only took five minutes. We were back on the highway, going an average of 28.3 miles per hour, according to Ed's bike computer. With the wind gusts, we would reach over forty mph

and once hit fifty mph as we got closer to Las Cruces. The wind and wind gusts were incredible.

At one point, Ed was going a little faster than me, and I had a hard time keeping up even though I was pedaling as hard as I could while being blown down the road by the wind. To pick up speed, I was getting frustrated biking in the rock, chip seal, cracks, and foreign object infested breakdown lane and started biking in the right lane of the highway, which had a very smooth surface. I started doing this for the speed, but I also did it because it seemed like most of the trucks were already leaving us the right lane as they passed us in the left lane. I could not see behind me because I did not have a mirror on my helmet, which meant I could not see if there were any vehicles behind me. A couple of trucks blew their horns at me, but not a lot, so I thought all was well until Ed stopped and pulled me over all of a sudden. He was agitated. He yelled at me, "are you crazy?" and "do you realize what you are doing?" I told him no to both questions. Ed then explained to me that when I was biking in the right lane, he could see the trucks get pretty close behind me before they would go over to the left lane. He said sometimes I caused a backup of trucks and cars because I was riding only thirty mph down the right lane. I felt stupid as I didn't realize how dangerous I was being and how I was causing difficulties for the truckers. We agreed I would stop biking on the right lane without his direction. Since Ed could see behind him with his mirror and the breakdown lane was not a good biking surface, I would follow Ed's lead when there were no vehicles in the right lane, and then when trucks or cars were coming, I would follow Ed's lead back in the breakdown lane. Our new tactic worked out well for both of us and was much safer. Ed was happy with this arrangement because he was very conscious of being a good bicyclist, riding safely with the truckers. I certainly respected his sentiment.

Just before we got to Las Cruces, a sign told us we had to exit at the next exit as bicyclists and ride a service road. It was quieter and safer with no traffic, but it was still very windy. We even biked by the Rio Grande River, which I was excited to see but surprised at what I saw. What looked like water was pure sand. It seemed surreal to have a park by the river with no water in it, only sand. I found out later that the Las Cruces area was experiencing a severe drought, and the water was redirected from the Rio Grande in the Las Cruces area to local farms.

After finally reaching Las Cruces by 1 pm, we started to head south, and that is when the substantial crosswinds made biking impossible. At one point, we started biking on the sidewalk because the road did not give us enough safe space from the cars as we kept blowing into the street. I was later blown off my bike when riding on the sidewalk, and I went for a tumble. Luckily, I was not out in the busy street. After just one and a half miles biking south, we stopped at a McDonalds to determine what we were going to do. It was only 1:30 pm, and we had already ridden 120 miles. I was only four miles south from a friend of a friend who said he would host me. However, we both came to the same conclusion that with sixty mph crosswind gusts, it was much too dangerous to bike, so we both got a room at the La Quinta Inn and relaxed for the rest of the day.

### Day 18 – (103 miles) Las Cruces, New Mexico to Fort Hancock, Texas

> "...I wish to live deliberately...I want to live deep and suck out all the marrow of life ...and not when I came to die, discovered I had not lived."
> – Henry David Thoreau

After a crazy day before, the early morning was cool, and the wind was still under control. I biked out of Las Cruces into pleasant, peaceful farmland where everyone seemed friendly as many people would wave to me as I was biking by pecan plantations and alfalfa farms. I thought it a bit odd that some guy just biking by at 7 am would get such favorable attention, but in reality, it fit the beautiful day.

I felt grateful for the opportunity to bike in such a beautiful place with the sun shining, the temperature was just right, and the biking was flat and comfortable. I was heading for Texas, which was hard to believe. It proved to me that biking a little bit every day was adding up, and I was already a thousand miles into the Southern Tier but knew that Texas represented a thousand-mile section itself and that was intimidating.

I made it to Texas just after 8 am, and there were all kinds of the hustle and bustle as people were driving off to work. Once it hit 9:30 am, and I was biking through the outskirts of El Paso, the wind started to pick up quite a bit, but it was mostly a crosswind and not as bad as the day before. I think I developed some strength and coping mechanisms from dealing with the crazy winds of the day before.

It turned out to be a typical day of riding as I was excited to get to the city of El Paso, but as soon as I got there and got caught up in the craziness of the city, I couldn't wait to get out. Thankfully, I had a cross/tailwind, and this helped me escape the city much quicker. I flew down a service road next to the highway that was along the Mexican border. I tended to think the border with Mexico was chaotic, especially with all the news about border walls and immigration challenges, but every border situation I had seen had been nothing but tranquility.

I ended up biking 103 miles, mostly because there was nowhere to camp. It seemed like the small towns along the border of Mexico were about fifteen miles apart, so if there were no good camping options, then you knew you were biking fifteen more miles. The winds were favorable and robust, so I didn't mind. I finally realized my last stand was Fort Hancock, and there was not much in that town. There was one motel about a mile and half off the road. I was wavering on my idea of not staying at a motel two nights in a row. I really could use a shower and a comfortable bed. I biked up the road to the motel. It looked dirty. It was the only option in town, and even though I thought it looked scary, I was still willing to stay. Thank god they were not open until 5 pm. I noticed the town hall just down the road, and I went in and asked the clerk about the best place for a bicyclist to sleep. She told me the best place was on the grounds of a church down the street that catered to bicyclists. She said I could camp anywhere on the grounds, and that it was a much better option than the motel. I found out later that the dumpy motel would have cost me $85 to stay the night, which was outrageous.

I set up my tent on the non-windy side of the church as the wind was blowing fiercely to the point it would be hard to set up the tent. The only problem with setting up on the non-windy side was that I was facing the street, and all the mosquitos congregated on the non-windy side.

A concern I had setting up my tent by the church had to do with leaving my food in my tent because the grounds I was camping on looked like a haven for raccoons. Normally, I never leave food in my tent due to the fact I do a great deal of hiking in bear country and a person should never leave food in a tent in bear country; however, since the beginning of the bike trip, it just seemed easier to seal my food in a dry bag, then put the dry bag in a sealed pannier, and leave it in my tent overnight. I had been counting on the double sealed food not producing smells that attract rodents nor animals. It was simpler and more convenient to have my food in my tent than leaving it in a pannier attached to my bike or hoisting it up a tree. Other than perhaps the Big Sur area there had been no areas with a bear population so the only animal I was concerned with were curious raccoons. Throughout my trip I had no problems with rodents or animals trying to get at my food in my tent. It was just that I was among lots of bushes and trees and the thought of a raccoon ripping into my tent in the middle of the night to go after my food scared the bejeebers out of me.

After setting up and cooking my meal, I settled into my tent. I noticed lots of townspeople walking, driving, and biking by as if I was some attraction. No one stopped by my tent to talk, but they kept their distance and whispered amongst themselves. I found out later that I was less than half a mile from the Mexican border and that Fort Hancock was the entry point into Mexico, after his escape from Shawshank State Prison, of fictional character Andy Dufresne from one of my favorite movies of all time "The Shawshank Redemption".

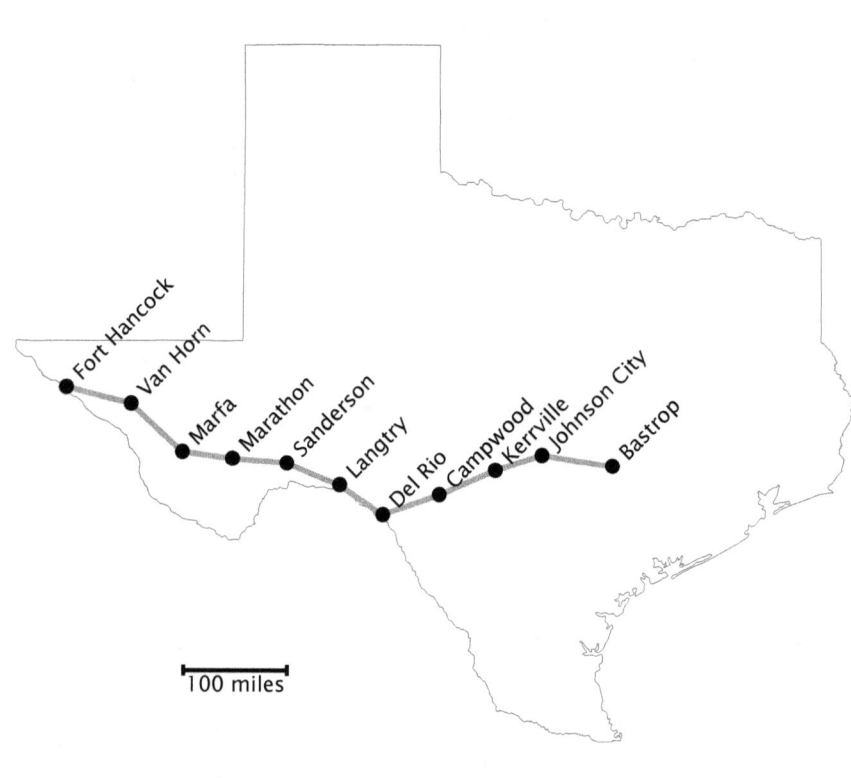

## Chapter 6: West Texas – Remote, Surprises, Hill Country

### Day 19 – (70 miles) Fort Hancock to Van Horn, Texas

> "What lies behind us and what lies before us are tiny matters compared to what lies within us."
> – Ralph Waldo Emerson

My day started with my first dog chasing me less than three hundred yards from where I slept. I was regretting I did not have any dog pepper spray as the dog was barking and chasing me for a mile. You never know what the dog thinks in that you don't know if it is some instinctual sport or they want to bite your ankle. I always consider the worst-case scenario.

During the chase, I kept my control and would ride on the other side of the road to get space. It was early and there were no cars. I sprayed my water bottle several times at the dog, and the dog would slow down but then speed up and catch up to me. I was not sure I was not more fearful at the time because I was still half asleep or that the dog was a big sheepdog and I wasn't that intimidated by it. After a mile, it finally gave up on me, and now I was sufficiently warmed up to start my day.

While the dog chase warmed me up, it also burnt out my legs. After two days of 120- and 103-mile efforts, my body needed a rest; however, I committed myself to bike to Van Horn 70 miles away. The ride to Van Horn would mostly take place on a busy highway with lots of trucks blasting by me at more than eighty miles per hour, which was the speed limit. Throughout the day, I was laboring as I just seemed to have no strength. I think I was not eating enough, and my fat reserve was gone. My lethargy got so bad that I was biking a slow 4 miles an hour up a 3% incline. I was so mad at myself for being so slow, but there was nothing I could do. The only town between myself and Van Horn was a tiny town called Sierra Blanca, and that was forty miles from where I started. It would be a miserable forty miles.

When I finally got to the outskirts of Sierra Blanca, I was having a near-death experience. I saw a fellow biker on the other side of the road, but I was so hungry that I just waved and kept going. I could tell he wanted to stop and talk; however, I was so out of it at this

# WEST TEXAS

point and desperate to eat anything that my sense of self-preservation dominated. I was hoping the restaurant at the other end of town was open. If it was open, I was eating there unless the restaurant was a total dump with rats and cockroaches running all over the joint. Once I got to the restaurant, I was never so happy to stop and eat. You don't realize what a privilege it is to eat until you are in such a desperate place. I looked over the menu and ordered the fattest meal I could see – country fried steak and eggs with gravy. I ended up eating it like a wild hyena on a juicy gazelle. A fly landed on my food as the waitress delivered it, and she went to whisk it away. However, I told her not to bother because I would eat it too. The waitress refilled my coffee cup so many times I thought she might get carpal tunnel syndrome. After the meal, I was fat and happy. I also probably sucked down a pot full of coffee and ended up leaving a big tip.

It took time for my body to absorb the nutrients, and I was still sluggish on my bike. However, nothing will get me more motivated and focused than seeing a red thunderstorm cell on my ACA map on my phone, descending on my destination town. The potential storm was just the motivation I needed to lose the lead in my legs and to bust a move to Van Horn quickly. I got to the town before it rained and settled into a very nice Motel 6 that gave me an excellent military discount. It was a beautiful place. Ed showed up an hour later, and we strategized about biking together the next day on the trip to the enigmatic Marfa, Texas.

## Day 20 – (74 miles) Van Horn to Marfa, Texas

*"The best thing about the future is that it comes one day at a time."*
*– Abraham Lincoln*

The morning started on the wrong foot as I noticed biking to the gas station to meet Ed that my back tire was pretty much flat. I berated myself for not seeing it earlier. At first, I thought of changing it, but I knew Ed wanted to get on the road, and I liked the idea of biking with Ed on a long-deserted highway in West Texas, so I got out my CO2 cartridge and blew air in the tire. It filled up in two seconds. The question was, "how dangerous is the flat? Is it a slow leak?" We would find out soon enough.

Ed and I got on the road just as the first light of the sun had breached the horizon. It was wonderfully crisp out, and we knew we had a straight, flat 74 miles on Highway 90 with no services to the funky town of Marfa. The ACA maps showed that their preferred route went through the Davis Mountains up to the McDonald Observatory; however, we had read that it could be raining in the mountains, and a local suggested that the alternate road Ed and I took would be scenic and dry. It turned out to be a great decision as the road was terrific to Marfa. We saw coyotes and antelope out in the ranch land. We were also benefitted by a good tailwind that helped us average 18 miles an hour to Marfa.

Thirty miles outside of Marfa is the craziest thing you will see in remote West Texas. There was a Prada storefront out of the middle of nowhere. Ed and I decided to take our break at the store. I guess the store was an art project that caught the imagination of America as the store has remained a tourist destination for twenty years. The store is tiny and does not sell items. It had cameras in the store due to past vandalism. It was funny to watch as carloads of tourists would stop by the Prada store and inevitably a boyfriend or husband would take the Instagram shot of their girlfriend or wife jumping in front of the Prada store like Beyoncé did on her Instagram feed.

As we continued, we saw a big balloon out in the wide-open fields that turned out to be a surveillance balloon for US border patrol. It

was relatively big and from what we understood, it used infrared cameras to scan for body heat in the search for undocumented immigrants coming from Mexico.

We arrived in Marfa by noon. I felt pretty fresh and contemplated joining Ed in continuing to the next town of Alpine; however, the weather looked like it could start raining and I had a Warmshower in Marfa for the night. In the end, I decided to stay in Marfa as Ed continued to Alpine.

My Warmshower host was surprised I rolled in early because he was not expecting me until later in the afternoon. I got to camp in his back yard, but I had no bathroom or shower facilities. I shared the backyard camping spot with another Warmshower guest, who had been biking throughout the US for two years. He was a great guy, a military veteran who decided to bike around the US indefinitely. He had all kinds of interesting stories to share. Later, he and I would have a great time checking out the local watering holes.

Everyone told me I had to check out the Marfa lights. The viewing area is nine miles outside of town. The Marfa Lights are mysterious lights that have shined outside town in a periodic, strange manner for the last 135 years. Unfortunately, it was very cloudy the night I was in town, so I never got to see the Marfa lights.

## Day 21 – (60 miles) Marfa to Marathon, Texas

> *"Every time I see an adult on a bicycle, I no longer despair for the future of the human race."*
> – H.G. Wells

It was 27 degrees when I woke up. The best way to beat the cold is to wake up fast and get warm clothes on as soon as possible, which means all the clothes I had in my pannier. All the fast movement makes you forget it is cold. Once I packed my tent and bike, I headed to a local gas station to get a large hot coffee to warm up.

I checked the weather, and it was expected to be cold in the morning but then warm up to mid-seventies by the afternoon. It was nice and warm in the gas station, but I knew I must get moving or I might get too comfortable and grow roots. Once on the road, it was helpful that I began the day biking uphill out of Marfa to warm up.

Biking in West Texas between Marfa and Marathon was beautiful country with well-maintained roads and low traffic volume. I made a quick stop at the Target (art display) store thirty miles east out of Marfa. It didn't quite have the impact of the Prada store that was west of Marfa. The Target store was vandalized and was smaller in stature. It made me think that Target was more modest in stature compared to Prada in more ways than one.

While I was grocery shopping in Alpine, I saw other bikers shopping for groceries. I found out they were part of an ACA bike group that was touring the Big Bend National Park area. Many of the bicyclists encourage me to meet the tour leader, and I said I would.

As I got on my bike, I realized I spent way too much time dillydallying in Alpine with my breakfast at McDonalds and shopping at the grocery store, so I was going to forgo meeting the ACA tour leader; however, as I was about to get on the main street in town that would take me to Marathon, I saw the tour leader at the edge of the grocery store's parking lot. I biked over to the tour leader, who looked busy organizing the food in his van. As I began talking to the tour leader, he seemed very familiar. He was amiable and was more than open to talk. As we spoke, I kept feeling like I knew the guy. I asked if he was on social media or YouTube and he said he had a YouTube channel. He mentioned he and his cousin had done a series of YouTube videos detailing their ride of the Southern Tier across the United States. He introduced himself as Johnny Lam of Milestone Rides. All of a sudden, a light bulb went off and I realized I was meeting Johnny Lam from the video series I watched before I left for my trip. I had just mentioned him and his wisdom over a beer in Marfa the night before. I was so flabbergasted at meeting Johnny, you would have thought I met Tom Cruise. Once I realized who he was, I started telling him how I was such a fan of his videos and how much they helped me prepare for my ride. I let him know I had been referencing his wisdom from his videos to other riders I was meeting since California. I think Johnny was a bit embarrassed and humbled by the effect his trip videos had on me. I even named off various videos I particularly liked. I seemed to remember his videos better than he did. It certainly made my day to meet him.

After meeting Johnny, I was certainly high from the experience, and it helped the miles melt away on my way to Marathon. It was Christmas again when I saw another bike tourist on the road riding from Big Bend National Park. He was an older gentleman who had been on many bike touring adventures in his life and has continued into his sixties. He was quite inspirational and made for great conversation. He gave me some tips on where to stay in Marathon, which included staying in the town campground and not the "unique" hostel even though it was a free stay. After a fifteen minute chat, we wished each other safe riding and headed on our way.

Riding through West Texas was beautiful: the roads were smooth, there was tremendous scenery with mountains, shrubs, desert, and the weather was perfect at seventy degrees and little wind. The winds wouldn't start until later in the day, but I would reach Marathon by 1 pm. It would be a shorter and relatively quick sixty mile day. I choose to stay at the main campground and pay the $20 fee as opposed to staying free at a local hostel. At the campsite, I bumped into Johnny Lam again, and we talked further about bike touring. It turned out that Johnny and his tour group of approximately fifteen riders would camp right next to me.

After setting up my tent, I then biked across the town of Marathon to check out the psychedelic hostel everyone had been talking to me about over the last few days. After biking down a dirt road for a mile, I got to the entrance to the compound that was the most unique hostel I had ever seen. It looked like something you would see in *Mad Max* or the *Flintstones*. The buildings were unique structures in and of themselves and all the buildings together made up a compound. It was hard to tell where the administrative office was located. I took a few photos and was amazed at the dedication it must have taken to build such a compound. It all looks rather old but in decent shape.

After a few photos, I got out of there quick as I didn't want to bring attention to myself.

As I biked back to my campsite, I recognized the beauty of the small town with the quaint houses, but I did notice some unique, quirky architecture that you might see at the "Burning Man Festival." Once I got into the downtown area, I stopped at a pub for lunch and ended up sitting with some of Johnny's tour riders for a beer. It is always fun to talk with other bikers about their adventures. They all seemed excited about biking to Big Bend National Park and they especially liked their tour leader Johnny Lam.

### Day 22 – (54 miles) Marathon to Sanderson, Texas

> "One of the greatest discoveries a man makes, one of the great surprises, is to find he can do what he was afraid he couldn't do."
> – Henry Ford

Today would start with a slow leak of my back tire. Johnny Lam let me borrow his tour group's super tire pump to pump up my back tire. I was a little concerned about losing pressure in the remote West Texas desert, but I took the chance. The tire has had a slow leak since Van Horn, but it did not seem to leak during the day. I decided to risk it and leave as soon as the sun popped out at about 6:30 am.

The ride started with very straight roads that were chip seal and bumpy. There was little traffic as I left Marathon, and I believe I was at the beginning of the hundred and forty mile stretch of West Texas where there were reportedly few places to get water or food. I planned to have lunch at a small town of Sanderson about fifty miles away.

While the road, the weather, and the wind were pleasant, I seemed to be lacking energy and noticed I needed to take a lot of breaks. During breaks, I tried to eat a lot of food, which included white powdered donuts, almonds, candy bars, and anything else I had in my bike bags, but I seemed to be always hungry. My attitude was also a little suspect as I could only think of stopping and taking a break and not looking at the positive in all the beauty that was before me. The highlight of my riding was having my imagination go wild when I saw an RV out in the desert and could only think of the show "Breaking Bad" as if someone was cooking up some meth (probably not but it was fun and an excellent mental exercise at the time).

Once I got into Sanderson, I was quite relieved to take a break. I find it hard to ride when I don't have a town gas station to break at once I am over thirty miles. At the Stripes gas station, I decided to buy two burrito meals that were only five dollars and may cause a severe gastrointestinal issue, but I was so hungry I did not care.

After lunch, I made an executive decision to stay in Sanderson at a cheap motel across the street from the Stripes gas station. I found out the next town was 60 miles away, and they had minimal services. It was hot, and I was tired. My body was telling me all morning I needed a break. Luck would have it that I bumped into another biker named Jeff who was also staying at the motel I was at, and we agreed to bike together to Del Rio over the next couple of days because the section of the Southern Tier we were on was deemed a dangerous part due to the remoteness and lack of services.

Dinner ended up being a pint of Haagen-Dazs ice cream and a small Pizza Hut pizza. Authentic gas station food that made me realize why people get a colon cleansing.

### Day 23 – (60 miles) Sanderson to Langtry, Texas

*"In every adversity lies the seed of an equal or greater opportunity."*
*– Napoleon Hill*

Jeff and I met in the darkness to walk over to the Stripes across the street to get breakfast and gather any snacks we would need for the day. I topped my water bottles, part of the six liters I had because I was deathly afraid of running out of water in a desert. I also had enough food for two days as we were likely not to see an open store until we were on the outskirts of Del Rio.

As soon as the sun was starting to light up the day, Jeff and I were off to Langtry. I appreciated meeting Jeff as he was 27 years old, intelligent, and a keen biker. He was great to talk to and miles melted away even though we were in a strong headwind for most of the ride.

The road was straight, hilly, but with little traffic. Very few vehicles drove by us, and due to this fact, we both recognized the same van had driven by us twice. We thought that was a bit odd, but what was even stranger, and surprising, was when a guy seemingly came out of the bushes on the side of the road asking me if Jeff and I wanted a ride because of the fierce headwinds. I looked over at his vehicle, and it was the van that passed us twice earlier. It had the back doors open and in the ready, for us to throw our bikes in the back. The gentleman was middle-aged, in his middle fifties, had a Texas drawl, and had on rancher clothes. He didn't seem like a threat, but you never know. I thanked the gentleman and laughed that we signed up for this ride, and the wind was part of the challenge. I told him I appreciated his offer, but we were on our way across Texas. I never did see his reaction as I never stopped as I had a good pace going and felt no need to change it. After I passed the gentleman, Jeff, who was a couple of hundred feet behind me, caught up to me and asked me what the guy wanted? I told Jeff, in a joking manner, that he was either a kindly West Texas gentleman offering us a ride or perhaps he was Hannibal Lecter's brother. We had a good laugh and carried on our way into the headwind until we reached the tiny town of Langtry.

After sixty miles, we saw that there was a small grocery store at the edge of town, but it was not open. We continued another mile on a loop road to the town center, where we were surprised to see the enormous, modern Judge Roy Bean Museum. It was a museum run by the federal government and appeared to be new. The museum staff was amicable and helpful. By all accounts, it was a very nice museum with lots of artifacts and a film made in the 1950s, which seemed very odd as the cars in the program were very old. It was strange that such a beautiful museum was in the town of thirteen people. At the time of our arrival, there were no stores, post office, or restaurants open.

Both Jeff and I were happy to be done for the day as the wind was ferocious and just drained the life out of us. I have to admit I finished strong but was ready to sit in the air conditioning of the museum.

We eventually made our way to the town community center, where we could pitch our tents for free. We had to set the tents on the west side of the building because the wind was fierce. As we were setting up our tents, an off-duty border patrol officer checked in on the center, and probably on us, to make sure everything was copasetic. The border patrol officer was friendly and told us that we were camping less than two thousand feet from the Mexican border. He said it was not unusual for undocumented immigrants to walk across the Rio Grande River and past where we were setting up our tents. The officer lived across the street from where we were camping and said he had had many undocumented immigrants coming from the Mexican border knock on his door in the past, not knowing who he was and that he worked for the US Border Patrol. He also said just the night before, not too far from our tents, Border Patrol caught five undocumented immigrants illegally crossing into the US. The border patrol officer was a wealth of information. You could tell he took his job very seriously and loved Langtry. Later, Jeff would ask him a few questions at his house as well as ask if he had any beer for sale after which he gave Jeff seven beers, which we much appreciated after a tough day of cycling.

Jeff and I drank the beer in front of the museum. The only people we saw were a couple of French-Canadian tourists looking for somewhere to park their RV for the night. We suggested the community center. Later, after talking with them a bit further, they were amazed that Jeff and I were biking across the US. They must have felt bad for us and gave us some fruit and yogurt to eat, which we much appreciated as we always seemed to be at a caloric deficit.

While we drank the beer, I noticed across the street was a Saguaro cactus that looked to be on steroids as it was huge with many large arms. I found out the next day from the museum staff that the cactus was illegally transported from the Arizona desert and planted across the street. West Texas can get a lot of rain, more rain than an Arizona desert, which is why the cactus had grown so large.

### Day 24 – (58 miles) Langtry to Del Rio, Texas

> *"It is our attitude at the beginning of a difficult task which, more than anything else, will affect its successful outcome."*
> – William James

Jeff and I negotiated to leave a little later than I liked to start because the weather forecast said the winds would die down later in the day; however, the estimates would turn out incorrect. The wind was strong when we left and would not relent the whole 58-mile ride. It also was hot, there were big hills to climb, and the only respite we had were shady rest area spots that we took full advantage. Jeff seemed a much stronger rider than me, as I wanted to stop at every rest area. All the stopping made our ride take much longer than usual and resulted in us riding during the heat of the day. My misery index was quite high as the temperature gauge hit 92 degrees. Jeff seemed unfazed by the conditions.

It was a rough day of biking as the heat and humidity were killing me. There was no convenience store for miles, and all I could think about was relaxing in an air-conditioned store drinking a Gatorade. After 46 miles of riding, I got my wish as we pulled into an Exxon station to take a break. As we pulled into the gas station, we talked about all the roadkill we saw and could smell. It was unusual. We both wondered where all the vultures were or public works to clean up the carnage. Jeff labeled the outskirts of Del Rio the "roadkill capital

of America" as we never saw or smelled so much roadkill in our two thousand-plus miles of riding.

As we were relaxing in the shade drinking our cold beverages in silence, an older gentleman in bike gear came up to us with a tremendous amount of energy as he asked us about our bike trip. The guy was so energetic and positive; I thought he was a reincarnated

Zig Ziglar. Usually, I love people asking me questions and having a conversation, but at this particular time, I was miserable. I tried to be polite and answers the gentleman's questions. However, the guy's enthusiasm was overpowering, and then we started asking questions about his bike ride. He told us he biked all over Del Rio and Texas every day. At some point, my ears perked up when all of a sudden, he said, "I've biked across the US before in twelve days". I thought "holy cow, twelve days!!" He then added he did it when he was 61 years old. What!! I asked if he was part of the RAAM, the bike race across America? And he said that he was and that he had completed the competition twice. He told us a rider would get disqualified if he did not bike at least 250 miles in a day, no matter what weather, wind, or illness would be occurring. As I thought about this, I thought about how I was dying after only 46 miles, and this guy biked 250 miles or more a day for twelve days at the age of 61. He encouraged us to look into doing distance races and gave us his business card. By the time the gentleman left, I felt energized. He wished us well and left on his bike. Jeff and I sat in the shade, wondering what hit us. He seemed more youthful than we were feeling at the time.

A few days later, I googled the name of the gentleman we met, and I realized Dex Tooke was a living legend in Del Rio. He was a member of the Ultra-Cycling Hall of Fame, had all kinds of cycling records in Texas, and was training to be the first 70-year-old to complete

RAAM in 2020. He wrote a book entitled "Unfinished Business: The Inspirational Story of True Grit and Determination" which chronicled his journey to finish the RAAM at age 61. It then hit me that Dex was 69 years old when we met him at the gas station. It goes to prove you never know who you will encounter while biking across the country. Once I had my wits about me, I thought, what a cool experience.

We were both stoked to stop riding as we split the cost of a suite at a cheap motel. We both were in dire need of a shower, to wash our clothes, and to eat a good nutritious meal that had nothing to do with McDonalds. We accomplished all of our goals, including eating at a Texas Barbecue place where I ate a pound and half of meat. It was delicious, and the protein filtered nicely through my muscles.

After we ate, the skies over Del Rio looked as if Armageddon was about to occur as it got very dark with scary-looking skies and even tornado warnings. It was frightening how dark it got. Jeff and I rushed back to our motel made of concrete and looked bombproof to escape the showers, winds, and lightning that were about to occur. While I decided to organize my gear in my room, Jeff thought it would be cool to sit by the pool and watch the clouds and lightning, which were putting on a show. I eventually joined him as the lightning was raging. Other motel guests on the second floor starting warning us to get inside because it was supposed to hail golf ball-sized hail; however, Jeff and I were hoping it would so we could experience it. Everyone thought we were nuts. Once it started raining huge drops, I went back into the room. The thunderstorm never did provide golf ball-sized hail or a tornado, but it did offer us some evening entertainment.

### Day 25 – (78 miles) Del Rio to outside Campwood, Texas

> *"The biggest adventure you can take is to live the life of your dreams."*
> – Oprah Winfrey

After an evening of eventful weather, I got up at 5 am so I could stop at Walmart to stock up on food and supplies then eat breakfast before heading east at first light.

It was fun biking with Jeff, but he wanted to take at least one day experiencing Ciudad Acuna, Mexico. I thought about joining him, but I was more motivated to head to Austin, where I could finally replace my duct tape shoe that I needed to periodically re-tape to keep it together.

This day would highlight how the wind can benefit and hinder your progress. The wind would remain consistent all day at 24 mph sustained winds with up to 38 mph gusts. The first 36 miles, I had a tailwind. The tailwind helped me complete 36 miles in 2 hours (18 mph), which was an excellent start to my day. However, after a break, I was headed northeast toward Campwood. The next 28 miles, I had a crosswind, which I found annoying but doable. I completed this portion even with the strong crosswind in a little over three hours for an average of 8.5 mph. The last part of the day's ride would be 14 miles into a frustrating headwind. It seemed like I could barely move into the twenty-four mph headwind; however, I could not stop to camp or take a break because there was nowhere to stop. Quitting to take a ride from someone was out of the question, so I embraced the suck and gutted it out. It is funny because I was very conscious of the misery I was under, but I seemed to embrace my situation and tried to make the best of it. I noticed my biking goals got a lot smaller as at some points when I was getting smacked by the 38 mph wind gusts, I was barely moving forward. My goals became to reach a phone post or mailbox or driveway. I thought in micro-goals and this seemed to propel me forward, even though the progress was slow. My mind continued to be in flow. I was thinking less of my misery and more about my goal. It also helped that as a strategy, I tried to keep my head down, looking at the white lane line to provide better aerodynamics with the headwind. I did look up periodically for vehicles, holes in the road, and dead animal carcasses in the bike lane. Biking over a dead animal could easily puncture a tire by biking over their broken bones. Also, biking over a dead animal is bad karma, and the blood, guts, and gore on your tire was nasty. The smell of death was also unappealing. I continued with my micro-goal progress for over three hours and was relieved to see a cozy-looking campground with a small convenience store. While my goal was to bike another five miles, I thought that the slow progress was a waste when I could wake up in the morning when the wind was less fierce and complete the last five miles in less than a half-hour.

In the end, even though the riding conditions were brutal, I was proud of myself for gutting it out, keeping a positive attitude, and coming to a great decision to camp at Wes Cooksey Park by a beautiful lake. The park was a peaceful sanctuary for me. A welcome respite after an eventful day in the wind.

### Day 26 – (87 miles) Outside Campwood to Kerrville, Texas

> *"Life is a great and wondrous mystery, and the only thing we know that we have for sure is what is right here right now. Don't miss it."*
> 
> *– Leo Buscaglia*

As expected, the wind died down in the morning, so the ride to Campwood was much more comfortable than it would have been the day before. Once I biked into the quaint town of Campwood, I made a spontaneous decision to eat a second breakfast after biking only five miles. I thought it was essential to build up my caloric reserve as I was heading into Texas hill country. There were some big hills in remote areas to climb, and the next town was twenty miles away. I could ill afford to bonk.

As I rode into the hill country, I began to notice the tremendous difference between biking on chip seal roads and smooth roads. Many of the side roads and bike lanes in Texas were chip sealed, which can get tiring for long-distance bikers because the road provides road chatter to your hands and arms, which eventually leads to fatigue. I found the chip seal annoying even though I have a big, heavy steel bike that cushions the chatter a bit. Due to the chatter on the chip sealed road, I would bike on the smooth road with little traffic on the road. While biking on the road, I wish I had a large bike helmet mirror so that I could see behind me at all times. I think with the mirror, my ride across America would have been smoother, quicker, safer, and ultimately, more enjoyable, especially when on chip seal bike lanes or roads.

Once I got to Leakey, I took a break and got an early lunch (to go with my two breakfasts after only twenty-five miles of biking). The ladies at the breakfast burrito stand where I was eating suggested I forgo biking the hills on the ACA route and take a more roundabout way to avoid biking in the narrow roads as they were not safe for bikers. Even Ed had texted me that the hills past Leakey were dangerous and made for uncomfortable riding. Ed had a lot of credibility, so when he said it was dangerous, then it was definitely dangerous. So, I heeded all the warnings and took the locals' suggested route. I was safer and better for it.

While biking the alternate way, my body, even with three meals, was sluggish. When I am fatigued, my decision making is not the same. For example, I decided I was getting hot, so I pulled over to take my bike tights off on the side of the road. While sitting on a guard rail, I planted my right foot on a red ant hill. Before I knew it, I had hundreds of red ants on my lower leg biting me rapidly – maybe that's why they call them "fire ants" in Texas. I must have killed three hundred ants trying to get them off my leg quickly. Due to my fatigue, I put my left foot on the anthill as I tried to take the ants off my right leg. My unfortunate incident was indicative of how slow my brain was making sound judgments and decisions due to fatigue.

Biking in Texas hill country was beautiful as the spring flowers were out, traffic volume was light, there were vast ranches with lots of deer and antelope in the fields, and plenty of entertaining hills. Biking the hills was like a game to me. I would use the momentum of going down one hill to try and make it up the next hill. The hills weren't necessarily long, but some of them could be super steep. What made the hill country a bit trying was the persistent east wind, especially in the afternoon, which would slow you down at all times. It was especially tough when you are on a flat section, and the wind slows your momentum as you hit a steep hill and then as you're climbing, you feel no wind as the hill is shielding you; however, as you crest the hill a twenty mph headwind slaps you in the face. The reward for going downhill with gravity in a headwind is you begin to slow down to the point that sometimes you had to stand and pedal to maintain your speed even going downhill. It was frustrating, but all part of the deal of riding across America.

Another biker and I debated what we liked better; the long three percent grade inclines for ten miles in the western states of California, Arizona, and New Mexico, or the rollercoaster ride of the Texas hill country. After much deliberation, my preference was the hill country because there is a quicker sense of accomplishment by getting to the top of the hill and knowing you're going to get to fly down the hill and, hopefully, use the momentum to get up the next hill. It was fun and made the day go by fast. It was more of a dopamine hit than say a very long continuous climb that could turn into a slog, and the downhill was just gradual. Ho-hum.

I got quite the surprise near Hunts, as I saw what I dubbed "boot art" on the side of the road. For over a mile on each side of the road were posts, about three feet apart, with an old shoe or boot on top of the post. It was humorous and interesting. It is funny, I saw other art along the side of the road that included old cars, various what appeared to be tractor parts, and different line-ups of junk displayed as roadside art. I guess it is true, "one person's junk is another person's treasure."

### Day 27 – (83 miles) Kerrville to Johnson City, Texas

*"The secret to happiness is freedom, and the secret to freedom is courage."*
– Thucydides

When I began this trip, I dreaded biking through Texas because it was a thousand miles across. I thought I would dread the scenery, the remote miles, and the never-ending struggle; however, I had been enjoying biking through Texas. I think the pleasant weather was a godsend. It also helped that I was getting used to biking eighty-plus miles per day, and I never felt bored. The people were wonderful, and the drivers were courteous to bikers.

I wanted to get out of Kerrville before it got busy, so I was out of the KOA by the time there was just enough light. I took a slight shortcut on a cutoff road designed to avoid the downtown area, and eventually, I was back on the road heading toward Austin. I had my bike tights on and was beginning to get hot when I started looking for somewhere to take off my tights that had no red ant hills. I saw a guardrail on an overpass to a busy highway below and leaned my bike on the guardrail. All I could think as I was taking my helmet and bike gloves off was "whatever I do, do not drop anything off the overpass," as there was a sixty-foot drop down to the highway. Sure, enough, just as I had the thought, I unsnapped my fastener on my Ortlieb bag, and my bike lock tumbled slowly off my Ortlieb bag, off the guardrail, over the guardrail, and onto the highway below. Luckily it fell onto the breakdown lane, and there were no cars or trucks on the road at the time. I couldn't believe that just what I was thinking happened. I kept telling myself how "stupid" I was to stop in the middle of an overpass. I eventually bushwacked through the thick brush, ran down the steep embankment, and retrieved my bike lock on the highway because it was a critical piece of equipment. Moral of the story going forward, never take a break in the middle of an overpass.

Once I got my bike tights off and fastened my bike lock securely to my Ortlieb bag, I continued my ride. I noticed I was on some bike route as I was meeting a lot of weekend riders in spandex and expensive carbon fiber bikes. I saw everyone took a right while I went straight. After one mile, I realized I was supposed to take that right. I was distraught with myself for making another dumb mistake in getting lost. Just as I realized my mistake, my second dog chase ensued as a small, yappy Chihuahua started chasing me with its little legs. The dog was determined to catch me and rid his territory of me. I easily outran it without trying and just laughed at the absurdity of the chase. At least I was laughing in the face of adversity.

Once I was on the established route as determined by my ACA Southern Tier map app on my phone, I looked ahead and saw the most prominent, steepest hill I had seen on the trip so far. In my mind, it was so steep it looked like a wall that spelled pain. My first thought was that there was no way I was biking up that hill as one, I would burn a lot of energy I felt I didn't have, and two, I might burn my legs out for the rest of the day

I was about to dismount from my bike when I heard a commotion behind me. I then realized I was on the route of a bike race. Those weekend warriors on carbon fiber bikes were heading for the hill, ready to scale it as fast as they could in their fifteen-pound bikes. As they started to pass and begin the climb, I did not want to look like a wimp, so I joined them up the hill. I thought my manhood was on the line, so I felt I must bike up this hill like a warrior even though I was on a thirty-two-pound steel bike with sixty pounds of gear on it. I took the hill as a personal challenge and quickly clicked into my granny gear and gutted out the steepest hill I ever climbed on my touring bike. I was undoubtedly huffing, puffing, spitting, grunting, and cursing up this hill as I did not want to look like a wimp to everyone. As I was cresting the top of the hill, I was about to have a heart attack when I noticed a car with a race official taking my picture. They yelled out how impressed they were that I was grinding it out. I didn't have the energy to smile or thank them because I was trying to hide my discomfort from my overexertion. I appreciated the words and only thought about the ugly-faced picture they must have gotten, but I was happy and impressed with myself that I made it up the hill with everyone else without dying.

After cresting the hill, my new-found confidence seemed to turn into cockiness as I began trying to race everyone on my fully loaded touring bike. Many cyclists were impressed I could keep up and even asked if I was training to bike across America? The question made me chuckle. What many of the riders didn't realize was that I was twenty-eight days into my cross-country ride and had completed many eighty-mile days, so I was powerful on my bike. While many of the riders around me were weekend warriors who worked all week sitting at a desk looking at a computer screen, but today, they could exercise their adventurous spirit on their light, fast, expensive bikes. For ten miles, I kept up with the back of the pack, but not the leaders. After reflecting on why I would do such a seemingly stupid thing as biking as fast as I could and keeping up with racing bikes was that it was such a different kind of riding than I had been doing over the last two thousand miles that I quite enjoyed it. I found it challenging. It got my adrenalin pumping and satisfied my competitive soul. However, all good things must come to an end. After I passed many of the main pack who stopped at a water station, I decided to slow down to a more leisurely ten mph pace so I would not burn out my legs. It was fun, and once I slowed down, I quite enjoyed the beautiful rolling hills, quiet roads, and the company of riders around me.

After approximately thirty miles of mixing with the racers, I biked into a larger picturesque town called Fredericksburg. There were lots of places to eat, but the traffic was quite thick. It was a touristy town but had a great deal of charm. I did stop at its McDonalds, an organic grocery store, and the local bike shop where the helpful owner helped me with a purchase of a new tire pump, 2 CO2 cartridges, and finally some HALT dog pepper spray, as I heard unleashed dogs chasing bicyclists was a problem in East Texas and Louisiana (which proved to be very real).

It would be another 35-mile ride to Johnson City up and down hills with beautiful pastoral scenery and periodic Texas longhorns grazing in the fields. I was excited to get to Johnson City. By the time I reached the small town, all I could think about was eating, so I found another fast food restaurant that was near the turn onto Robinson Road that then led to Austin. I was glad I choose that fast food restaurant as I spent an hour with locals who had a lot of questions about the ride. It was good to talk to someone after being on my bike by myself for so long. It is funny: I was so tired as I biked into Johnson City that while I was craving a Subway sandwich, I didn't have the energy or resolve to bike the extra half a mile up a slight hill to get to the Subway. I was into conserving what little energy I had left as I had a little under ten miles to go to reach my Warmshower host.

My Warmshower host gave me directions to her place that included taking a left onto a dirt road, biking down the dirt road for a mile and a half, find a wagon wheel, and turn left into a driveway to look for a red house. My imagination started going wild again as I was asking myself why I trusted this person to host me. I felt vulnerable that I was so off the beaten path in a remote area. Visions of Kathy

Bates in *Misery* kept floating through my mind again as I thought my Warmshower host could be a sick serial killer or something. But then again, the Warmshower host could think I am an ax murderer on a bike. So, people wonder what I think about while I am riding, and as they can envision, my imagination, especially when exhausted, can go in all kinds of directions. In the end, my Warmshower host, like all my Warmshower hosts on my trip, was terrific and a cool person who just happened to live in a remote place down a long dirt road and loves to host adventurous bike tourists.

Once I got to the place, my Warmshower host was not home, but she had told me to look for the red house. At first, I saw a red shed and thought what am I getting myself into as it didn't look comfortable at all, but as I walked around the property, I saw a pretty, red tiny house that looked striking out in the field. When I opened the door to the tiny house, it was even cozier and more beautiful inside. I felt I struck gold as it was an excellent place to stay. It had both a ceiling fan and an air conditioner. It also had a reading chair and a big window. My host had instructed me to read the directions provided in the tiny house. The detailed instructions told me how the electricity worked and where to shower. I noticed I barely got any internet service but had just enough to make my daily Facebook post about my journey.

I enjoyed the tiny house and my host was very accommodating. Later while I was relaxing, as it was getting dark, I was reading on the comfy chair provided when I looked out the window and spied a fox looking for food just outside my window. I could tell it could not see me, but I could see it. It was cool spying on nature. Later the next morning, when I had to pee after waking up, I opened my door, and I had a field of deer in front of me to greet the morning. I could get used to all this beautiful nature in front of me. The only aspect of the cabin I did not like is if I had to go #2, I had to use the bucket provided, with a toilet seat on it. A benefit was that the toilet bucket was portable so I could do my business wherever I preferred, but I had to throw the results into the garden and rake it into the soil as well as wash out the bucket. It was one time I was feeling glad to be constipated during my stay.

## Day 28 – (88 miles) Johnson City to Bastrop, Texas

> *"And, when you want something, all the universe conspires in helping you achieve it."*
> *– Paulo Coelho*

While my stay at the tiny red house was excellent, and I had great sleep, my body seemed to want to rest on Easter Sunday. There was little traffic on the roads, but some of the hills I was hitting were very steep, and I seemed to have low leg power. Nowhere seemed open, and I was in a dire need for a large breakfast. I thought I should be able to make it to Austin by noon to meet Ed, but I severely underestimated the hills and my lethargic physical condition. Even though I pushed myself and sometimes pushed my bike up some of the big climbs, I was not going to make Austin on time. I still needed to stop at the REI in Austin to get my bike checked as my rear cog was skipping, and my brakes needed new pads. I also needed to buy new bike shoes to replace my duct tape shoe and a new sleeping mat as I had accidentally rammed my fork through my inflatable mat, rendering it useless.

Ironically, I am always excited to bike to a big city, whether it be San Diego, Phoenix, or Austin; however, as soon as I get to the city and I see the crowds and the traffic, I can't wait to get out. Austin, to me, is a very hip city with a progressive vibe and great music, but I was only interested in getting my bike fixed, going shopping for needed supplies, and biking out of Austin as soon as possible. Once I got to the REI in Austin, I stopped by the bike shop counter to ask my standard question about whether they do emergency repairs for people biking across the US? Especially if they are riding an REI brand Novara Randonée? The bike shop said they did and dropped everything to service my bike. After a quick analysis of my bike's working condition, the bike mechanic told me I had a rear cog that was missing teeth (which is why my bike was having trouble staying in gear), and I needed new brake pads in the front and back. The repairs took a little over an hour and cost me $135. My bike worked great after the repairs, and I was confident that it would be in good shape for the last fifteen hundred miles. While in REI, I also checked out bike shoes. Surprisingly they did not have my style shoe or shoes in my size, so I needed to continue biking with my duct tape shoe. I did pick up a new inflatable sleeping mat so I could sleep in more comfort in my tent.

I was back on the road at 2 pm, and onto the crowded bike paths of Austin on Easter Sunday. It was a typically beautiful day in Austin, and all the Austinites were out soaking up the eighty-degree weather and blue skies. I biked through the center of town, and then another biker on a carbon fiber bike started talking with me. I found out his name was Bruce, and he told me he had organized and selected the trails on much of the ACA bike route through Texas. It was great to bump into him because it was a little confusing biking through Austin, but he showed me the way and we talked about biking across the US. He biked with me for about twenty minutes and pointed out the road that I should go down and gave me a couple of camping ideas in the area. He was a good dude who turned out to be super helpful.

As I made my way down the busy streets of eastern Austin, I can tell I was in a lower working-class area as the streets weren't as clean, the car stereos were louder, and there seemed to be more rough-looking characters around. I never felt unsafe, but I did feel a need to be on my guard. I stopped at a 7-Eleven to get a Gatorade and a candy bar and relax a bit. There were what appeared to be gang bangers in the 7-Eleven with their hard looks, tattoos, and gang swag. They parked their fancy cars with the huge wheel rims in front and left their loud stereos on to let everyone know that they were in the neighborhood. I walked in as I walked into any other convenience store. Everyone looked at me like I was different and in the wrong neighborhood. I could tell some of the people I walked by were thinking I was crazy, and I wasn't sure whether they wanted to buy me a beer or kick my spandex-clad ass. However, like everywhere else I went, some of them inevitably had questions about the bike ride and were surprised I came from California. It seems like no matter who I talked to, whether they be truckers, Apache Indians, gang bangers, or little old ladies, they all seemed to be intrigued by my ride, and many of them had the same general response about my adventure – "that it was bad ass."

I left the 7-Eleven, and even though I had had a thirty-minute break, I was dragging. I seemed to be lacking the energy or resolve to complete a big day of riding. I wanted to be out of the city as quickly as I could. Unfortunately, Austin is pretty spread out, and my destination was Bastrop, which was still thirty-five miles away. I remember I kept stopping at convenience stores and felt I needed to eat a substantial meal. Subways were closed because of Easter Sunday, so I had to feast on mostly candy bars and Gatorade. I even stopped at a cheap motel, but the price would be $100 for a night, and I didn't feel it was worth it, so I continued onwards. The headwind and traffic certainly did not help my motivation. Later I would get lost for the fourth time that day, and I was close to being fed up, but there was nowhere really to stop. At some point, I believe it was after I ate a couple of bananas instead of a candy bar, I got my second wind, and all of I sudden it seemed like I was superman again. It must have been the potassium in the banana instead of the sugar in the candy bar. Within no time, I made it to Bastrop. It would be an 88-mile day that included a long stop for bike repairs and shopping in Austin.

I stayed at the Bastrop Inn. Since it was near shopping, I stocked up on food and other essentials and did all the little things I needed to do to prepare myself for what would be a big day the next day. People who do not bike across America do not realize how much logistics and preparation goes into each day, especially for a self-supported ride. I spent a good hour and half plus cleaning up my bags and bike, shopping, cooking a second dinner of spaghetti and tuna because the first dinner at McDonalds was not enough, fixing my bike, checking my tires for goat heads (a thorn that can pierce your tire), checking the weather for the next day, planning for the next day including where I might end up, sleep, and eat, check funds, check cash, check wind, etc. I didn't end up going to bed until 10:30 pm, which is at least two hours later than my usual bedtime when I am at a motel.

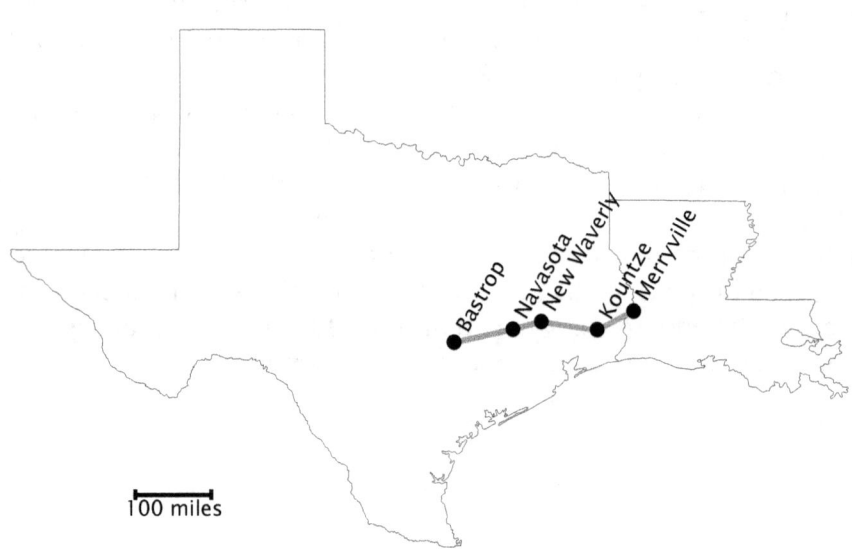

## Chapter 7: East Texas – Dogs, Thunderstorms, Tornados

*Day 29 – (108 miles) Bastrop to Navasota, Texas*

> *"Character is like a tree and reputation like a shadow. The shadow is what we think of it; the tree is the real thing."*
> *– Abraham Lincoln*

Once I made it up a big hill with trucks blasting by me two feet away, I turned into a state park for the next fifteen miles or so. The park turned out to be very hilly. Many of the hills were very steep. I would take a "walking break" up the hills so I would not burn out my legs too soon because I was planning a hundred mile day. All the hills were annoying, and I didn't think the state park was all that attractive given the state parks I am used to in Washington state (perhaps I am a bit of a nature snob).

I would end up riding 108 miles mostly through ranch country. I was sluggish most of the day again and just seemed hungry and lethargic. As I was grinding out miles and recovering after being freaked out by a couple of dogs chasing me earlier in the morning, I looked ahead and saw another medium-sized dog, who looked fast, not on a leash, waiting for me to get to the driveway he was guarding. I initially biked over to the other side of the deserted road. However, I was fed up with being chased by dogs. So I immediately reached into my handlebar bag, got out my dog pepper spray, looked straight at the dog that seemed to be waiting for me, raised my arm with the dog spray in my hand, and yelled out "say hello to my little friend" (just as Tony Montana said as he locked and loaded his supergun as his foes surrounded him in his final scene in the 1983 classic movie *Scarface*). I said it with the most authoritative, loud voice that I could with my eyes closed because I said it with such power. I opened my eyes, looked towards the dog, and the dog sprinted for the back of the house. He wanted nothing to do with me. I had never seen a dog run so fast. Later, when I posted on my Facebook page about my day, I stated that either the dog was intimidated by my authoritative voice or the dog and its owner had watched "Scarface." I am sure readers thought I was dishing hyperbole, but was I?

So far, on my trip, I had seven dogs chase me, and when I yelled "go home" at them, I might as well have yelled, "eat me, I am a steak" because they never slowed down and kept coming for me. Most dogs I was able to outrun because I was going downhill. It was easy to beat an ill, stray dog that was too weak to keep up. Then there are dogs with short legs. They are all barking and snarling but had no speed. Good times.

Just before I got to the small town of La Grange, I was hot and hangry, and I needed to get in the shade and drink some water. My lack of calories and dehydration were slowing me down. I didn't feel like I could eat or drink enough. As I was biking and still recovering from my last dog chase, I was purely miserable when I glanced to my right and saw a donkey. I glanced again and saw a herd of fifty donkeys galloping towards me from across a fence line. I remember thinking I had never seen so many donkeys together in one area, and they were all coming towards me. I kept telling myself to stop to take this unique picture, but I was so hot and hangry I decided to forgo the unique photo and head for a big oak tree a half a mile down the road. As I biked for the oak tree that promised shade, water, and a break, I thought I should have taken a picture of the donkey herd coming at me so I could have posted it on my Facebook page with the caption "What a bunch of asses!"

As I got closer to La Grange, I saw that there was a Whataburger restaurant on the edge of town. Whataburger to Texans is what In-and-Out Burger is to Californians. My friend Andrea told me that I would like it and it was much better than McDonalds. Once I arrived at the restaurant, I was so relieved and excited to eat because I was famished. A bonus was I bumped into Ed, who I hadn't seen since we biked together to Marfa. He was leaving as I was locking up my bike. We shared some notes, especially about dogs chasing us, and wished each other the best on our journeys. We would keep in text contact throughout the ride. By the way, I must say Andrea was right, Whataburger was delicious and way better than McDonalds. It also could have been that I was so hungry that I could have eaten roadkill and loved it.

Later, when I finished my ride, I found out that only a few days after I passed the area, the area of La Grange was hit by a tornado which took out a few barns.

After a long lunch break, I still had over 64 miles to go before I got to Navasota. My goal was Navasota because it was only 43 miles from New Waverly, TX, where I was going to meet a friend I had not seen in 23 years. I was excited to see her. So, it was worth a big day today to have a more relaxed day tomorrow.

The hills were a little gentler, but the miles were not as I struggled to reach my goal. I saw lots of cattle ranches, some more Texas longhorn cattle, private oil drilling, or perhaps fracking activity, lots of vultures including one particular scene of forty vultures taking turns on a fresh deer kill that looked like something out of a documentary on Africa. The funny thing about vultures is that they are a massive bird that look powerful but are chickens because they would always fly away if you got to close to them no matter how delicious the carcass they were feeding on.

A good strategy I utilized when I was struggling on my bike was to use mile-marker rides I had done in the past as beacons of hope. For example, if I was six miles from my destination and I was struggling, I would just think the ride was like biking from work or if it was four miles then it was like biking home from Bellingham Center. Even on longer rides of twenty miles, I would think about how it was twenty miles down Chuckanut Drive to Bow, Washington for pie and this thought would get me thinking of a positive experience and make the next twenty miles seem very doable. Forty miles would be from my house in Bellingham to Bow and back, which I had done many times and loved it. Even elevation could come into context with rides along the rolling Chuckanut Drive, up five thousand feet to Mt Baker's Artist Point, or over Washington Pass toward Winthrop, Washington. If I was struggling on my bike, mind games and good bike memories would distract me from my hunger, lethargy, and negative thoughts and help pull me through to my destination.

By the time I got to Navasota, I was exhausted. I decided to forgo the free camping in town. I got a cheap motel that looked like a horror show on the outside, but the inside was adequate. It felt good to stop pedaling.

### Day 30 – (42 miles) Navasota to New Waverly (stayed in Conroy, Texas)

> *"People will forget what you said, forget what you did, but people will never forget how you made them feel."*
> – Maya Angelou

I woke up excited because I knew I had a short day and would be staying with a college friend. It is probably not surprising that I had a hard time waking up, but I was determined to stick to my routine of leaving as the sun was starting to light the day.

After just biking a couple of miles outside of Navasota, I had another dog chase me, but the funny part is I did not realize it at first. While I was biking up a slight gradual hill on a relatively busy road, passing cars and trucks were honking at me. Initially, I thought they were friendly, and I would wave at them but after the third person honked at me I began to think something was wrong, so I checked my clothes, then my face to see if something was on it, I had my helmet on, and then I looked at my panniers to see if anything was out of place as I was riding up the hill. As I took a double-take, I saw a scruffy looking sheepdog chasing me, but it was not barking. Since I was concerned with how close the dog was to me, I quickly reached inside my handlebar bag for the dog pepper spray. I had used this pepper spray before in Bellingham, and it worked well as the savage dog that was chasing me was hit with a short burst warning shot, and it quickly stopped. However, on this day, I noticed my new can of dog pepper spray (called "Halt") sprayed more of a mist than a medium stream. The problem with the spray was that it was not concentrated enough to bother the dog, so when I sprayed the dog, the dog hesitated for a second but then quickly caught up to me. I sprayed the dog three times before it finally gave up the chase. The dog looked dirty and may have been a stray dog chasing me out of its instinct. It was always scary to have a dog chasing you because you never know if the dog is going to try to bite you or run you off the road.

After lunch, I became more focused as I was biking by large ranches and sweeping vistas. The hills were becoming shallower, and I had come to the realization that I was on the downhill slope of the trip and barring a severe bike issue or crash I was going to make it. It also helps to know that you were seeing a friend from your past, and you were going to be sleeping in a comfortable bed after a warm shower and eat a large meal with lots of protein.

I was done with my ride by noon and had about three hours to kill before my friend Cami Davey arrived. Cami was a super trooper by getting out of work and driving an hour north to pick me up in downtown New Waverly. It was awesome to see her. We caught up with each other's lives, reminiscence about graduate school, wondered where all the time went, talked about our friend Rich Carvajal, and generally enjoyed each other's company. She was a Dean at a local community college and loving it. After dropping my bike and gear at her lovely house, we took a tour of her campus as only higher education professional geeks love to do when visiting friends who work at a college. Cami was aghast that I was still biking with a duct tape shoe and was adamant we find new shoes to buy. Even my friend Rich texted he would throw in a few dollars for my new shoes because he knew I was such a cheapskate. In the end, the stores we stopped by didn't have my style, my size, or the shoes were too expensive, so I ended up continuing with my old shoes but did put a new round of black duct tape that would last to the Atlantic Ocean.

After a great meal and time with her family and friends, it was time to sleep in a comfortable bed. I appreciated Cami's hospitality. Cami did get on me about not fixing my slow leak that I was too lazy to fix, which turned out to be a burden the next day. I also told Cami that I had not decided on taking a zero-day until I checked out the forecast in the morning.

It is important to note that I was always checking out the forecast and trying to figure out how not to get wet or stuck in a thunderstorm. There is nothing worse than getting stuck out in the middle of nowhere with high winds, thundershowers, and lightning other than having a tornado touch down in front of me. These were all possibilities over the next several days, so if I could outrun the weather, then that is what I would try to do. In my case, that might mean not taking a zero-day and furiously biking as many miles toward Louisiana as I could to get in front of the coming storm.

### Day 31 – (84 miles) New Waverly to Kountze, Texas

*"Worry never robs tomorrow of its sorrow, it only saps today of its joy."*

– Leo Buscaglia

The alarm rang at 5 am, and I went straight for my phone to check the weather. Accuweather revealed that thunderstorms and potentially tornados were forecast later in the afternoon, especially in the area I was biking. One concern that riders don't think about is that thunderstorms can flood the roads, and the highway patrol can close the roads for days until the flooding subsides. While biking east of Austin, I saw plenty of signs of flooding on roadway signs, especially where there was a dip between two hills or a nearby river or stream. I thought about whether I would try to ride through a flooded road, but this could be dangerous in regards to the deepness of the water, the hidden current, and snakes.

My decision was not to take a zero-day in order to try to outrun the wet weather forecast, so Cami drove me back to New Waverly. After a warm hug with Cami, she was off to work and I stopped in the convenience store for the last snack and another coffee as it was still too dark to ride. Once sufficiently fueled up and I could see a little, I was off heading for Louisiana.

It was great riding weather as the temperatures were in the seventies, it was cloudy, no wind, and little humidity. About an hour into my ride, I looked up ahead to a group of road work crews looking at me funny. When I looked over at a driveway where they were working, I realized they were wondering how I was going to handle three big dogs awaiting my arrival. Luckily, I had good forward momentum as I saw the dogs and immediately kicked into high gear and flew by the dogs who started to chase me but I had so much speed that two gave up quickly and the one starting to chase me didn't have a chance as I was biking downhill with lots of energy. On this particular day, I would have six incidents of being chased by dogs. Ed was texting me, as he was ten miles ahead, about potential dog encounters. My standard question was, "are we talking Cujo (mean dog) or Benji (friendly dog)?" Most of the time, it was a Benji dog, but still, it will scare you to see any kind of dog ready to chase you.

For lunch, I stopped at Subway, and the young twenty-year-old sandwich maker was very interested in my ride. He said he would love to join me, but he found it hard to bike across town. I assured him that if he wanted to bike across the continent, he could with the right preparation and equipment. He then asked me my age, and when I told him his response was, "wow, you're in great shape for your age! I thought you were a lot younger except for your grey hair". I took it as a compliment – I guess. While talking to the Subway employee, I again was having a weak moment and was seriously considering getting a nearby motel and calling it a day. I still had about forty miles to go, and it looked like it was going to storm at any moment. In the end, my goal for the day was more powerful than my weak mind.

Within ten miles, I started to have my first real rain of the trip. I had to get out my raincoat and biked with it on for about two hours. The rain soaked me, so I took an extra-long break at a gas station and drank a large hot coffee to warm up. It was a good idea because when I stepped out of the coffee shop, it had stopped raining.

At my gas station/convenience store stops, I noticed I must have been feeling more comfortable (or just being lazy) as I stopped locking my bike up. Instead, I just left it outside the store as no one ever paid attention to it. It could be because I am out in the country. At the beginning of the trip, I locked my bike every time I stopped including when I was camping. Being that I grew up in the city and have had three bikes stolen, I pretty much didn't trust anyone; however, as I biked the second half of my journey, I rarely locked the bike. This kind of thinking also extended to strangers. Initially, I didn't try to talk to strangers as I had trust issues; however, as the ride unfolded, I relaxed more and took the time to speak to the locals who always seemed friendly and curious. It was the friendly people I would meet during my trip that made the trip more rewarding. I found it more satisfying than the scenery and the actual challenge. That is saying something.

The last few miles of the day, I started noticing all kinds of bugs flying into me, mostly hitting my face. It was good I had sturdy sunglasses as a big moth smashed into my right eye, a speeding bee smashed into my left cheek, and I do not know what kind of bug but it was rather large as it split my lips and smashed into my teeth. I quickly pulled it out by its legs with the help of my right-hand's fingers and spit reaction – nasty. In this case, my teeth saved me. I realized I better keep my lips closed tight.

The last twenty miles were dealing with my slow leak that was becoming a fast leak. I should have listened to Cami and had my slow leak fixed at her house. However, I was too lazy, and now I was paying the price. Every five miles, I had to pump air into my tire.

At one point in my enthusiasm to pump air into my flat tire, I once again stepped on a big red ant hill and paid the price with several itchy bites. I eventually fixed the slow leak I had since Van Horn, about eight hundred miles earlier, in my motel room. It only took twenty minutes to replace the tire tube. Again, I should have done it at Cami's house, but I always like doing things the hard way.

After 84 miles, I was finally in Kountze, and I registered in the first motel I saw – the Relax Inn. I wanted to camp that night to save some money, but the forecast was for heavy thunderstorms and possibly tornados. You don't want to be in a tent in those conditions.

### Day 32 – (63 miles) Kountze, Texas to Merryville, Louisiana

> *"Failure will never overtake me if my determination to succeed is strong enough."*
> – Og Mandino

It stormed out all night, but according to a local, I just missed the terrible weather. As I walked out the door of my motel room, it was clear skies, but still very wet outside. I decided I would delay leaving in case there was standing water on the road and would look for a place to eat a big breakfast. Across the street from my motel was a unique looking establishment called Mama Jack's Roadhouse Café. It looked like a Texas eatery out of Hollywood. I noticed there were only pick-up trucks out front. As I entered the restaurant, there were lots of friendly locals, so I felt comfortable that the locals thought enough of the food to eat at the establishment. It certainly didn't look like a Denny's as there were heads of deer and other game on the walls. I perused the menu but the waitress strongly encouraged me to order the all-you-can-eat buffet. I looked over at the buffet, which I usually do not like because of experience in some restaurants where all the food is old and looking disgusting; however, one look at Mama Jacks' buffet and I was sold. It all looked fresh, and they had massive freshly baked cinnamon rolls cooling on the counter. As I devoured three plates of breakfast and one large cinnamon bun, I was thinking that the last thing the waitress should have done is suggest to a cross country bike tourist who was famished and running a caloric deficit to eat as much as he could. I also drank a ridiculous amount of coffee. I was like a kid in a candy store. I must have eaten 4000 calories and felt I needed a tow truck to get myself out of the restaurant. The restaurant owner was happy to see me leave and to think I only paid $11 for all that food and coffee! My calories per dollar quotient was very favorable. I felt like the picture I remembered from childhood of a snake that ate a goat. I probably didn't need to eat for the rest of the day.

In an ode to the odd, while eating my breakfast, I glanced to my right and saw a sign for Mama Jack's Roadhouse Café on the wall. That was not unusual; however, what was surprising was the Tony Montana from Scarface sign below it. Yes! It proved perhaps the dog and its owner from a couple of days before did see the Scarface movie after all.

I waddled over to my motel and prepared my bike to set off a little later than I usually do at 8:15 am. Once I jumped on the road, the riding was phenomenal as the roads were flat, no wind, the air crisp, and there were good bike lanes. The only problem I had concerned the fact I drank so much coffee at Mama Jacks, I had to pee bad.

There was no place to pee, and I didn't feel comfortable with what I usually did in this situation, which was pee from my bike on the side of the road because the roads were too busy. So, I held it until the next town, which I believed had a lot of service stations and even a McDonalds. Unfortunately, I had to go so bad that I stopped at the first convenience store I saw. However, for the first time since I was a baby, I couldn't hold it as I was trying to lock my bike. I started briefly peeing in my bike shorts and had to hold my manhood to stop it. I quickly just dropped the idea of locking my bike and felt secure enough to run into the store and find the bathroom. I had my left hand holding my manhood that was stopping my urine flow behind my handlebar bag I held with my right hand, but when I asked where the bathroom was because I had an emergency, the young clerk said the words that came to me as a shock, "They had no bathroom." I was so shocked by the news, my system let go, and I peed my bike shorts some more, and a few drops hit the floor. I was now officially mortified and was in acute distress. I grabbed my manhood even harder to try to stop the flow, praying for a miracle. I think I said something to the order of "I am desperate" as I tried to stop from totally relieving myself on the floor in front of the clerk. The clerk, who was on the phone talking to a friend, all of a sudden realized my situation but I think she thought I was going to shit my pants and didn't even know I was actually only peeing my pants (I never asked if she knew what was going on) but judging from her wide-eyed looked she must have seen my desperation and realize it was dire. She quickly said there was a bathroom at the laundry across the small parking lot, so I quickly shot out of the store like a rocket, which seemed to distract the issue, and bolted to the laundry's bathroom where I could finally relieve my discomfort.

After the incident, I was a bit embarrassed and wondered what I should do about my wet bike shorts. After three seconds of thought, I realized that ultra-bikers and adventures who stretch their physical limits pee and shit their pants all the time, so in reality, it is not unusual. Perhaps I could reframe my incident as having now joined the club. Yes! That made me feel better. It brought up a memory of a guy from Bellingham who told the story in front of a large audience about how he shit his pants while attempting to break a Guinness Book of World Record. He was quite detailed in his explanation, and believe me, my situation was benign compared to his condition. However, I did not go into the convenience store to buy a coffee. The thought of seeing the young clerk again horrified me. I could only imagine what she was saying to the person on the other end of her phone call. I quickly jumped on my bike with my wet bike shorts and continued to ride as if nothing happened. The shorts dried soon in the heat and wind.

After my situation, I biked by a McDonalds for the first time all trip and did not stop. Part of the reason was I was still full from Mama Jack's and the other reason I was still embarrassed about what happened and just wished to bike far away from the incident.

I concentrated on getting to Louisiana. As I was riding, I saw a dead four hundred pound boar on the side of the road. The boar was huge, and I could only imagine the damage to the vehicle that hit it. I heard wild boars are a massive problem in the south, and I can see why because they are large animals with an attitude.

Also, while riding in the southern states, I would also see lots of big and small dead snakes (thank goodness!) in the breakdown lane including a venomous copperhead with its distinct pattern.

It seemed surreal once I saw the sign, "Welcome to Louisiana." When I was planning the trip, I was a bit overwhelmed with the distance. The fact that it was a thousand miles to get across Texas made me seriously doubt I would ever make Louisiana. However, there I was looking at the welcome sign. Wow! I couldn't believe I just crossed Texas. For the next ten miles, I thought about the feat of biking over twenty-five hundred miles at this point and was feeling very confident I was going to make it to the Atlantic Ocean.

I was staying in Merryville, Louisiana for the night because there was a Warmshower host. Once in Merryville, I called my host, who was part of the local historical society. Most bike tourists camp on the historical society's lawn, but since there was quite the thunderstorm the night before, the grounds were very soggy, so they offered to let me to stay in a storage shed behind the county stage. At first, I was a little concerned, but when I looked inside, it had a bed, a table, and an air conditioner. It turned out to be a great place to stay.

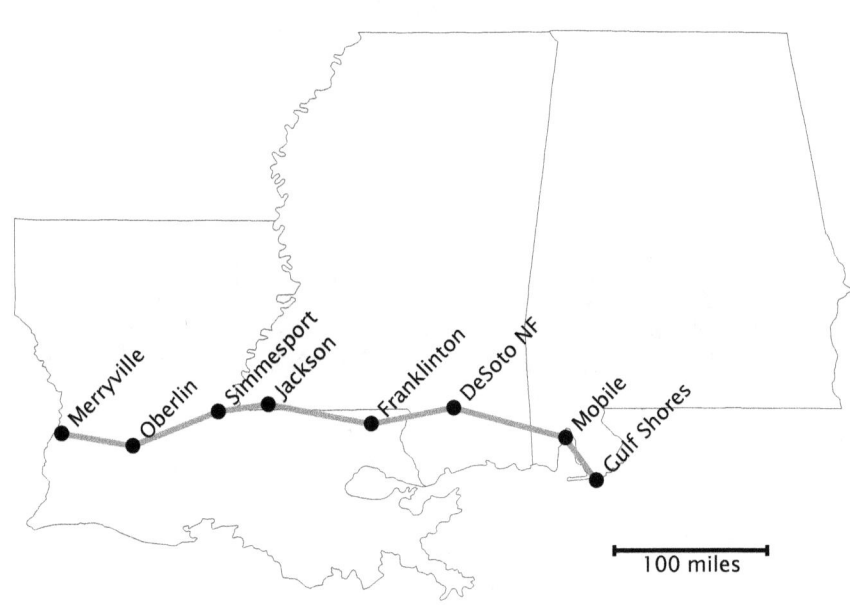

# Chapter 8: The South (Louisiana, Mississippi, Alabama) – More Dogs, Warmshowers, Lovely People

*Day 33 – (56 miles) Merryville to Oberlin, Louisiana*

> *"If you truly love nature, you will find beauty everywhere."*
> *– Vincent Van Gogh*

There is a beautiful peacefulness about early mornings in a small town with no one around. I realize I am the only human alive experiencing it at that moment. There is a sense of hope it is going to be a great day, and I can't stop smiling.

I started my day with a strange sighting. I looked to my left and saw a dog house in the middle of a pond. Why would there be a dog house in the middle of a pond? I couldn't come up with a good reason and only chalked it up to "this is Louisiana." I posted the picture on my Facebook page with the heading "either Rover likes to swim, or they have a pet alligator?"

The bike riding was quite delightful, and I enjoyed not having one dog chase me all day. I was diligent in having some serious situational awareness as if I was in the dangerous streets of a combat zone. I heard all kinds of rumors about loose dogs in Louisiana and the south. It wouldn't be true until the next day when all hell would break loose.

The highlight of my short ride for the day would be meeting Jose "Lil Joe" Chapa at a McDonalds in DeRidder. At first, I just concentrated on devouring my big breakfast, but I noticed this younger guy with a briefcase and laptop out sitting at the table next to me. We started talking, and I was impressed that this young guy turned out to be running for Sherriff of his parish. From listening to his story, it sounded like something out of "Walking Tall," where he felt there was corruption in town, that many townspeople, especially from underrepresented groups, felt marginalized, and the town needed change. Lil Joe wanted to be that change, so he put actions behind his words and thoughts. What surprised me was that he was only 18 years of age, but he was serious about winning the election. We ended up talking for an hour, and I was impressed with his gumption and sincerity. He was certainly on a different adventure, and I wished him well.

After I left, I thought about how I meet so many interesting people from all walks of life at a McDonalds or during breaks. After having a conversation with the locals, it gives me something to think about as I am biking, and it helps me to enter a state of flow. The miles biked melt away as I ride in bliss.

During my last Gatorade break of the day, I bumped into a local who could not believe I biked from California. He was so overwhelmed with the thought, he kept saying I was crazy and wondered why I would do such a thing. While the sentiment wasn't surprising, as I had heard it from others, but what made this encounter ironic was that the middle-aged, southern gentleman all of a sudden stopped with his incredulous comments, paused, and then shared that he was crazy too because he liked hunting for days out in a swamp or remote woods. Hunting for turkeys or deer or whatever with thousands of mosquitoes, snakes, spiders, and rain for days just for the sport and to maybe catch dinner. It was as if he had a revelation to the secret of life. His summation was that "we all have our crazy thing we do" and it makes life interesting. So, at the end of our conversation, he summarized that my trip was not so bad after all and that he admired me for pursuing my "crazy thing".

It was a short 56-mile day, and I had another Warmshower stay. This time I got to set up my tent in the park behind the Allen Parish Tourist Commission. My hosts were super friendly, and one even drove me to the local eatery to get my second dinner and drove me back to my campsite. The park was in the center of a small town, and like most small towns in the south, it had a Dollar General. I had no idea what a Dollar General was, so I walked over to see what they sold. It caught my attention that candy bars were 85 cents and a bag of Hostess white powdered donuts were $2. Cheap food but not necessarily nutritious. Good cheap eats for now but not good for my health in the long run.

Once it got dark, I went to bed. Some riders might explore the town at night, but I was not that kind of rider. I liked walking around town when the sun was up, but once the sun started going down, I was all about going to bed early so I could wake up early.

Over the last couple of weeks, I began to notice that due to all the mileage I was riding I would wake up in the middle of the night with sore legs that were very tight. Several times a night, while I was sleeping, I would have to "stretch and flex" my legs for a minute or two so the tightness would stop waking me up. It felt as if my body was shriveling up (perhaps a part of my aging process) while sleeping and I needed to "stretch and flex" to make my legs feel normal. It had me thinking that perhaps I needed a pliability massage advocated by TB12 Therapy that has benefitted Tom Brady of the New England Patriots with extending his career as he aged. A periodic full body massage would be nice while biking across America!

### Day 34 – (106 miles) Oberlin to Simmesport, Louisiana

> "The happiness of your life depends on the quality of your thoughts."
> – Marcus Aurelius

Barking dogs and freight trains ruled the morning hours, which was not conducive to a good night sleep. I couldn't understand how anyone in town got any sleep with all the noise.

The rough night's sleep set the mood for the day. As I left my campsite, I saw a street full of dogs just hanging out, looking up to no good. I was praying they wouldn't see me and start giving chase. I biked as quickly out of their sight as I could, and I succeeded. During the day, twelve dogs chased me. Ed, who was ahead of me, would be chased by sixteen dogs. Dogs would come out of yards, driveways, and bushes. There would also be scruffy stray dogs coming from out of nowhere. The dog situation was getting so bad that I was experiencing PTSD moments as any movement of any kind, whether it was a bird or a falling leaf in my periphery, was potentially a dog coming at me. Some dogs chased me with the owner watching, and it upset me that they wouldn't say anything to their dog. My dog spray was not very useful, and yelling at the dogs didn't do much for me. A couple of dogs almost got hit by a truck. By the end of the day, after biking over eighty miles and hearing there were even more dogs ahead, from a text I received from Ed, I decided to bike the last few miles on the main highway.

Other than the dog situation, I found biking in Louisiana beautiful as it was lush, flat, and had many large farms. The towns were small, and the people were friendly. The first town I biked through was Mamou. It was known as the "Cajun Music Capital of the World" and home to the world-famous Fred's Lounge. I stopped in Mamou to have breakfast and then walked across the street to Fred's Lounge as they were setting up for their live Saturday show that started at 9:30 am. It was surprisingly crowded but was not my scene, so I took a mental note, a few pictures, and was back on the road.

The next town was Ville Platte, which Ed deemed a dangerous place as he had stayed there the night before. As I rolled into town, I saw lots of sporty cars and trucks with expensive rims like you would see on the show "Pimp My Ride." The music was blaring with heavy bass, and the occupants of the vehicles looked hard like gangbangers. There was not a friendly, safe vibe to the community, and I felt uncomfortable leaving my bike out front of the gas station while purchasing some junk food. I agreed with Ed and couldn't get out of Ville Platte fast enough. Once out of Ville Platte, the roads were smooth and flat; there was little wind and blue skies. It was excellent biking conditions. Other than being chased by many dogs, I enjoyed my ride. I did have a rather large crawfish want to fight my bike, even out in the middle of the highway. I took its picture as it chased me. It was a warrior.

I ended my day after biking 106 miles at a restaurant, Rabalais Seafood, my Warmshower host. I knew of the Warmshower spot because Johnny Lam and his cousin had stayed at this Warmshower and enjoyed it, so I wanted to experience it as well. I ate an excellent pork chop meal and then went to set up my tent behind the restaurant. Out back was the owner's dog, who was a giant furry white dog that loved to jump up on you and hug you. It was the sweetest dog I saw all day. Initially, I was going to sleep behind the restaurant, but my host offered me the option to sleep in the restaurant after closing. So, I set up my tent in the restaurant. When my host saw what I was doing, he was shocked and said no one had ever set up their tent in the restaurant in the twenty-five years he has been hosting bicyclists. They usually roll out their sleeping bags, sleep, and then leave in the morning; however, I told my host I set up the tent because I do not like bugs of any kind and feel much more secure in the cocoon that is my tent. He was okay with it, but I did have to move some tables around to fit the tent.

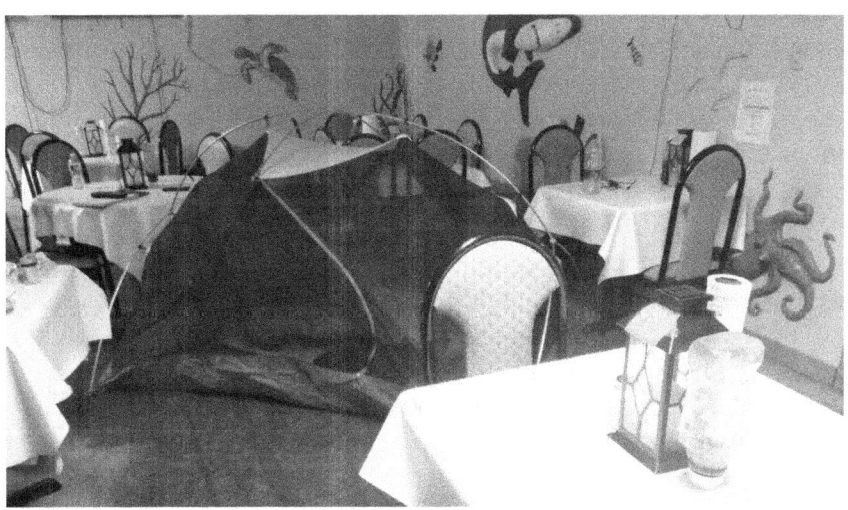

## THE SOUTH (LOUISIANA, MISSISSIPPI, ALABAMA)

### Day 35 – (51 miles) Simmesport to Jackson, Louisiana

*"A journey is best measured in friends rather than miles."*
*– Tim Cahill*

The first thing I noticed as I started riding was the swarms of gnats that were so thick, I could hear the staccato sound of them crashing into my hard raincoat as I biked forward. From talking with friends in Georgia, they had warned me about the gnats and no-see-ums in the spring. I was kind of concerned about dealing with them for the rest of the trip because I did find them incredibly annoying, but the further away from Simmesport I rode, the less I saw or heard them.

I started my ride by biking across the big bridge with no bike lane over the Atchafalaya River very early because there would be a lot of trucks on the road later in the day. So I biked as fast as I could until I was ten miles out and only slowed to a more normal pace when there was finally a bike lane. I again stuck to the highway to avoid charging dogs.

It was Sunday morning, and it was great riding in the fresh air, with no traffic, and the knowledge I had a rather short day ahead of me. I headed for New Roads to see if I could eat breakfast, but once I biked into the small community, I noticed it had the small southern town feel and was predominantly African-America. Since it was Sunday, many people were in their Sunday best coming from church. Amazingly, there were no restaurants that I could see, so I resorted to the convenience store for junk food and the Dollar General for spaghetti sauce across the street. I checked my map, and there was a larger convenience store that served burgers about twenty miles away, but before I hit the store, I had to cross the Mississippi River.

There is always something intimidating about seeing a massive bridge and then passing over a significant landmark like the Mississippi River. The river itself was quite extensive, and the views from the bridge expansive. It appeared the river was running over its banks.

I finally reached the gas station that served burgers. It was not the fanciest place, but I needed the fat. I felt desperate. It was fun talking to the locals as they all had questions about biking across the US. It was like I told them I was a space alien as they could barely believe me except for the fact I looked a bit dirty and very fit. The store manager, a trucker, and a guy heading for a rodeo all wanted to talk and take pictures. It was fun to listen to their stories and their perspectives about biking across America.

My last stop of the day, after just 51 miles, was my Warmshower host Perry Templeton's home. It was just south of Jackson in the middle of the woods. I was told to look out for an old bike in front of the driveway, so once I found it, I biked up the long driveway and met the Templeton's who were the friendliest people. They told me they host between two and four hundred bicyclists a year. On this particular day, I was the only cyclist, so I had individual attention. The Templeton's had a structure set up just for bikers. It had an open sleeping area where I was initially going to sleep, but since I hate bugs, I decided to set up my tent on the deck. The structure had a bike repair area, sleeping area, and on the side, the most refreshing, hottest outdoor shower. The grounds were beautiful as Perry had many bird feeders that attracted all kinds of birds, including cardinals, woodpeckers, various songbirds, and, unfortunately, hawks. Perry sat with me and gave me an education about the birds of the area that included sound effects. I also found out that Perry was very knowledgeable about the area lizards. Later I would walk the grounds with Perry to check her motion sensors to see what kind of animals were running around on her property. She said she had seen many deer, fox, and a bobcat, but she was especially interested in seeing the wild boar that dug up part of her property. We did not see any boar. While I had many excellent Warmshower stays on my trip, staying at the Templeton compound was the best because of the excellent facilities, education on birds, lizards, and area animals with Perry, and the healthy dinner she made me that featured black rice. Staying with Perry was relaxing for the body, mind, and spirit.

## THE SOUTH (LOUISIANA, MISSISSIPPI, ALABAMA)

### Day 36 – (78 miles) Jackson to Franklinton, Louisiana

*"Youth is happy because it has the capacity to see beauty. Anyone who keeps the ability to see beauty never grows old."*
*– Franz Kafka*

It was hard to leave Perry, but after saying no to the second cup of great coffee, I jumped on the road at my usual time and headed towards Mississippi. The roads were busy initially because of the changing shift at the local prison. I decided again to forgo the route suggested by the ACA map because I didn't want to deal with dogs and decided to stay on Highway 10. Perry suggested I remain on the highway because it was quicker, more scenic, fewer hills, and no dogs. She was right! Also, after about twenty-five miles, I made it to Clinton where a mile off the road was a McDonalds. It seemed like any reserves I may have had in my body were now depleted, so I needed to eat constantly to maintain my energy.

After breakfast, I was back on Highway 10, going east when I decided to take a Gatorade break in Greensburg. I walked into the convenience store, and the store manager was super friendly. He had lots of questions about the bike trip and was very talkative. As I was looking around his shop, I saw a sheriff's deputy stop by to tell the store manager about the rash of armed robberies of convenience stores in the neighborhood. The deputy also shared what the assailants were driving and described them. It concerned me as this was the first known danger I heard about, but I was amazed at how calm the store manager was about the news. He did look like someone who could handle himself. As I was getting ready to leave the store, a customer, Shondra, and her boyfriend walked in and started talking with the store manager. The store manager introduced me to Shondra, and she was amazed at the fact I biked from California. She asked me what I ate for fuel, and I gave her my standard answer of "this body is fueled by McDonalds" as I showed off my svelte body. Shondra was very surprised and quickly said, "hell no, this body (her body) is fueled by McDonalds" and showed me her curvy figure. We both laughed, and to prove to Shondra of my credibility and addiction, I told her I had breakfast at the McDonalds in Clinton. We both laughed again. Shondra was also amazed at how dark my skin was, especially my legs, and she put her arm next to my leg and declared me half black (as she was African-American) because my legs were much darker than her arm. Again, we both laughed. After a few more questions, I declared I had to go, and we wish each other the best.

I realized it was surprising visits with the locals like I just had that made the trip even more special and rewarding than I thought the trip would be for me.

As I left the store, I continued to have in the back of my mind that there were a couple of criminals driving a late model Honda Civic robbing stores but hopefully not bike tourists. I slowly biked into another town twenty miles away, and it seemed very rough and run down. The convenience store was scary to go into as the clientele, hard-looking men looking depressed, gave me long stares that made me feel both fortunate but also uncomfortable. My intuition told me to get out of town fast, so that is what I did even though I was famished again. Safety trumped hunger in this situation.

My Warmshower host for the evening was the Franklinton Police Department. I wasn't sure I was staying in the police department because they were super nice or because it was the safest place in town. I didn't think Franklinton seemed unsafe. The police were very friendly and willing to help out bike tourists. I was asked to set up my tent out in the back of the police station in the grassy field that included their tactical equipment. I heard that if it was raining hard, I could sleep in the interrogation room in the police station. I took a nice warm shower at the station and cooked my meal in the officer's lounge area. It was weird to walk freely in and out of the police station and then walk back to the tactical area where my tent was set up, but the officers seemed used to it. In the police station, I was known as "the bike guy."

## THE SOUTH (LOUISIANA, MISSISSIPPI, ALABAMA)

### Day 37 – (96 miles) Franklinton, Louisiana to DeSoto National Forest, Mississippi

> *"And into the forest I go, to lose my mind and find my soul."*
> *– John Muir*

If there was ever a time, I wanted to shoot a bird it was this morning from 3:30 to 5:30 am when a rooster kept letting me know it was morning because they confused the bright lights of the police station for the sun. The noisy rooster kept going and going and waking me up. Even when I finally got up and it was still dusk, it was still making noise. The second surprise of the morning was the three hundred miniature snails on my tent. It was extremely humid all night, and my tent was very wet with all these snails clinging to my rain fly. I could bat some of them off, but I then had to pick off the rest. It is not an enjoyable chore for someone who hates bugs or snails of all kinds. It slightly delayed me from leaving, but I tried my hardest not to pack some away with my tent.

I jumped back onto Highway 10 towards Bogalusa, Louisiana, to avoid dogs. Since I did not have any more dog pepper spray, I didn't want to take the risk of a dog biting me. Once I got to Bogalusa, I liked saying the name of the town as it rolls off my tongue, I found a Walmart and bought the only pepper spray they had that was suitable for dogs and humans.

With my new-found confidence in dealing with dogs, I decided to go back to the designated ACA Southern Tier route and ride on the more rural roads. The roads were great to ride on. However, I noticed some roads had overflowing lakes or rivers that drove into the forest and created a moat along the side of the road. It appeared as if one good rainstorm and the road would be inundated with water and not passable. It is seeing roads like this that concern me, especially with the threat of thunderstorms.

I would have a long 96-mile day and not see one dog. During the last twenty miles, I did bonk again, but I had a bag of white powdered donuts to the rescue. My endpoint was the DeSoto National Forest, where there was a beautiful campground by a lake that was free, but once I got there, it had a note posted saying it was closed due to a fishing tournament five days away. I had looked forward to staying there. I was struggling and was in the wrong frame of mind; however, when in this state, it did not pay to get too frustrated as it would drain the little energy I had. There appeared to be another campground eight miles away that was on the grounds of an old World War 2

German POW Camp. I had to bike a mile down a dirt road and found an open field that looked like I would be able to pitch my tent. I noticed a couple of RVs out in an open area that could have been a parking lot. One was playing loud music, drinking heavily, singing out loud, and had an unleashed dog running about the grounds. I was concerned about the behavior and felt a bit unsafe. I tried to pitch my tent as far away from the RVs as I could with some bushes blocking the view of each other as they didn't seem like the friendliest of neighbors; however, after biking 96 miles and being tired and hungry, I just went with the flow. I didn't let my loud, drunk neighbors bother me. I was too tired to care, but I kept my pepper spray near me just in case. My biggest concern camping where I was were the armies of red ants that were around my tent. I did kill twenty-five red ants in my tent that arrived on my shoes. I thoroughly checked the inside of my tent for more before I fell asleep.

### Day 38 – (63 miles) Desoto National Forest, Mississippi to Mobile, Alabama

> "A true friend is someone who thinks you are a good egg even though he knows you are slightly cracked."
> – Bernard Meltzer

It was very humid out as I got back on the road, and I had to take my glasses off because they kept fogging up. It was good riding on the chip seal roads, and there was no traffic. It was quite remote, and I enjoyed the fresh, humid air hitting my face. I was in a happy mood because I felt safe being out of the free camping area I stayed in last night, and I knew I was visiting a friend at his house in Mobile, Alabama, who contacted me on Facebook and offered me to stay with him when I was in the area. He was only ten miles off the path and very well worth a visit as I hadn't seen him in seventeen years since I was his supervisor at the Brown University Summer Studies program.

Bike riding every day seemed to be getting more comfortable and natural. There were fewer hills that were challenging, and the miles seem to go by faster. I felt more confident than ever that I was going to finish, and this confidence propelled me forward.

Biking through Mississippi seemed to go by fast, and before I knew it, I was in Alabama. Alabama lacked biking infrastructure. There were no bike lanes, more people beeped at me and yelled at me to get off the road, and I didn't find biking in Alabama very fun. I couldn't wait to get out of the state. Luckily, I would only be in

Alabama for a day and a half. My favorite part of riding in Alabama was finding a small country store where I got a Gatorade (or two) and relaxed in a rocking chair out front. I sat in that comfortable rocking chair for over an hour. My goal for the day was to see my friend in Mobile, but he and his wife were working and would not be back to their home until 3:30 pm, so I had lots of time to kill. I killed it rocking in a rocking chair.

I finally biked the last ten miles of the day to my friend's house, and it was great to see Scott after so many years. We spent the rest of the day catching up on our lives. I met his wife and children and learned about the eight-acre compound that his house sat on. Scott showed me his super sitting lawnmower that helped him cut his seven-acre lawn in five hours. He asked if I wanted to ride the lawnmower and look for big snakes on his property. While it sounded cool and very southern, I thought I would pass and relax. Scott's wife cooked us a wonderful, healthy meal of chicken with vegetables. My body needed vegetables and pure meat instead of fast food. We had a great evening catching up. After a great meal, excellent company, and relaxing time, I realized it was just what I needed to recharge the batteries for the last five hundred miles of my journey. The end was near, and I was feeling great!

### Day 39 – (66 miles) Mobile to Gulf Shores, Alabama

*"Obstacles are the raw materials of great accomplishment."*
*– Tommy Newberry*

Wow! The power of friends on the road is unreal as Scott took me out for breakfast at his favorite place in Mobile. I, unfortunately, or perhaps, fortunately, succumbed to the second cup of coffee with Scott as I did not want to leave his company. The more time I spent eating breakfast with Scott meant less time and a smaller margin of error, to catch the 11 am ferry from Dauphin Island. I still had 30 miles to bike, and I ended up leaving myself only three and a half hours to make it.

Once Scott dropped me and my bike off back on the ACA route, I started to bike like a man possessed towards Dauphin Island. I was determined to make the 11 am ferry because I wanted to make it to Pensacola, Florida, by the evening. Luckily, the area I was biking was flat, and the roads were good. The only frustrating part was the terrible headwind I was fighting, but the area I was biking was beautiful with lots of bayous and tremendous scenery. I was in the middle of the Shrimping Capital of America, and I had this feeling I was in the middle of the "Forrest Gump" movie when Tom Hanks had his shrimp boat. I wanted to take pictures to immortalize the scene, but I was too focused on catching the ferry.

Biking over the big bridge to Dauphin Island turned out to be a beast because of the thirty mph sustained headwinds. As I was biking down from the apex of the bridge, I was biking only two miles an hour. I could walk my bike faster. My attitude in this predicament was surprising positive as I felt comfortable at this point that I was going to make the ferry, although it was going to be a miserable riding experience.

Once I arrived at the ferry dock, I was forty-five minutes early, so I decided to buy lunch. The ferry ride was very comfortable as we speed through Mobile Bay in between many oil docking platforms. Sea birds flew alongside us, the sun was warm, and there was a sense of accomplishment in making it to the ferry considering my late start and the terrible headwind.

Once on the other side, I thought I was in Florida, but apparently, I was still in Alabama for another twenty-five miles. I started noticing my bike was having some severe gear issues, and I could not get any power on my pedal strokes. The chatter coming from my chain was disturbing, and I was debating whether I was going to make it to Pensacola. The gear issues, along with the continuous headwind, was putting a damper on my biking enthusiasm. I realized I was getting very frustrated with my bike, and I needed to stop to see if I could repair my gear issue. Unfortunately, there seemed to be no available camping where I was, so I decided to get a cheap motel in Gulf Shores, Alabama for the evening. At my motel, I tried to fix my bike to no avail. My priority the next day was to get my bike fixed, but the bike shop I was targeting was over fifty miles away. I hoped my bike would last that long as it sounded terrible.

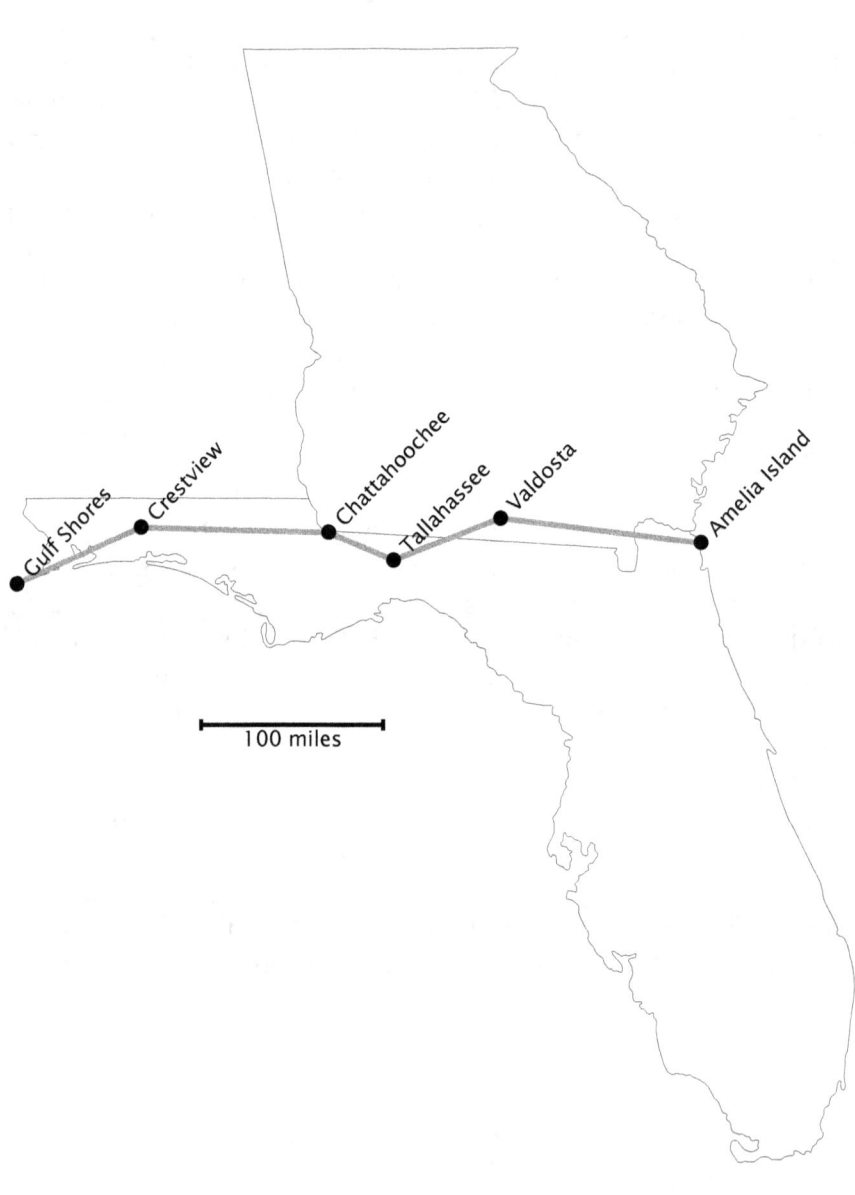

## Chapter 9: The Southern Tier Bicycle Route Ride Ends (Florida, Georgia, Florida) – Food, Gratitude, Accomplishment

*Day 40 – (98 miles) Gulf Shores, Alabama to Crestview, Florida*
> *"The real voyage of discovery consists not in seeking new landscapes but in having new eyes."*
> *– Marcel Proust*

It seemed unbelievable that today I would hit my last state (not really because I would bike into southern Georgia) and that being Florida. I had visions of biking along the beaches of Pensacola, but this was not to be because it was foggy out as I reached the Florida border. I couldn't see much. It was weird because the fog made it seem like I was biking in another dimension. With the quiet of the morning and the thick fog it seemed like I was on a psychedelic acid trip. The last person on earth. It was a unique riding experience.

Since I started super early thankfully there wasn't a lot of traffic. I heard some horror stories about biking in Florida, but there seemed to be a good biking infrastructure, and people seemed to share the roads well with bikes.

One thing I realized as I get closer to finishing my ride is that I now required eating two large breakfasts a morning. The big breakfast I had at McDonalds was 1350 calories, and after thirty miles, I found a Waffle House and ordered a steak and egg breakfast with a large OJ. While my breakfast at McDonalds was $8, my second breakfast at the Waffle House was $15. With all the food I was consuming, I realized that I would be spending twice as much if I continually ate at a Waffle House as compared to McDonalds. The quality of the food, while slightly better at the Waffle House, was not as important to me as the fat content needed and the cost. No more Waffle Houses going forward and more McDonalds (unfortunately).

I couldn't understand how someone could bike across America as a vegan or vegetarian. I think part of my problem with needing so many calories was due to averaging eighty miles per day. Salads and the like would not cut it as I was probably eating close to five thousand calories per day, but I was still ravenous and would find out I had lost 18 pounds during the bike trip.

Ever since I left Austin, the miles seemed to melt away, and any trepidation I had with biking across America had dissipated. I loved the simplicity of life on a bike in that I had a clear mission, I was using my body to accomplish the task, and any given day promised lots of mystery and challenge. I owned my success and failure. To me, failure was not an option throughout the 3,411 miles of my ride. While I still had fears concerning getting caught in a wicked thunderstorm or my bike breaking down, I was not going to let it stop me. If anything, I was getting stronger every day, and even when I hit the Atlantic Ocean, I felt I could have just kept going around the world.

While I was feeling strong biking through Pensacola, my bike was having serious issues as the gears kept on skipping. I saw on my ACA phone app map that there was a bike shop in Milton, along the route, and I planned on stopping there to see if they did emergency bike repairs. As I walked into the bike shop, the mechanic looked very busy. I asked the mechanic my magic question concerning emergency bike repairs for people biking across America, and especially so close to finishing, and he responded very favorably. He dropped what he was doing and quickly put my bike on his mechanic stand and asked me what was going on. I was amazed at how fast he worked, and he diagnosed the problem within fifteen seconds of me describing the problem. He told me it appeared the rear fork my derailleur was attached to, part of the frame, was slightly bent, which caused the gears to be out of alignment. The repair sounded expensive and possibly unfixable; however, the mechanic, without skipping a beat, picked up a tool from his bench, that looked homemade, and said no problem, we'll bend it back. Within fifteen minutes, the mechanic had diagnosed the problem, disassembled my gears, bent back the fork with his funky tool, reassembled everything, and got the gears working like new. I couldn't believe how skilled he was at his craft. He was very impressive! I asked how much I owed him. I was stunned when he said since I was biking across the United States, the repair was on the house. I thanked him. He did amazing work. It amazes me that I was biking the whole time with a bent rear fork and that I was not getting efficient power in my pedaling. I might have finished my journey even faster with proper gear alignment.

Biking through the pine forests and straight, flat roads of Florida were a joy. The miles went by fast. It seemed more natural for me to get into a flow state while riding without too many terrain challenges. I was always aware of thunderstorms and was continuously checking the weather and storm patterns to try and escape biking in the rain. If I had to bike faster or farther or stop riding early to miss a significant rain event, I would do it.

I ended up staying at a cheap motel in Crestview. The weather was looking a bit unstable, and tornado cells were in the area, so I was glad I was staying in a motel built with cinder blocks and concrete. The place seemed like a bomb shelter, especially with the shower you had to step down into and was fully enclosed. I felt like I was in a submarine, and it seemed like the perfect place to be if a tornado showed up outside. No tornados would show up, but nasty thunderstorms and lightning did, but I slept through it.

### Day 41 – (110 miles) Crestview to Chattahoochee, Florida

> *"To be yourself in a world that is constantly trying to make you something else is the greatest accomplishment."*
> *– Ralph Waldo Emerson*

As I stepped outside to start my day, I noticed it was very wet, and the skies looked ominous. I was very concerned because I had a big bike day planned as my Warmshower host was a hundred and ten miles away. The weather was for thunderstorm threats all day. I would be 100% focused on getting to where I needed to go. I was motivated to get out of the red thunderstorm section on my map app before 1 pm. The cumulous-nimbus clouds that seem to spontaneous grow in the sky in front of me were also very motivating. The sky looked grey and full of potential to wreak havoc as I set off.

With the darkening skies, I tried to prepare myself mentally in case I got stuck in a bad rainstorm. I did have my rain gear that included booties and a Gore-Tex rain hat that makes me feel like I am in a cocoon when I do get stuck in heavy rain.

In case I needed a reminder of how weather can devastate a community, I biked through Marianna, which had been partially destroyed by a category five hurricane just six months earlier. It appeared the town still had massive storm damage. In some of the parks, all the trees had been blown down, most houses had blue tarp roofs, and many homes and businesses still had debris piles in front of their driveways ready for pickup. It looked like the aftermath of a war zone, but the community was slowly cleaning up and getting back to normal. However, on the day I was biking through, they were battening down the hatches as another bad thunderstorm with potential damaging wind and hail were forecast to roll through. I had terrible visions of being pelted on my bike with golf ball-sized hail. It was thoughts such as those that kept me focused and helped me bike through my lactic acid laden legs to get to Chattahoochee.

Once I crossed the Chattahoochee River, and after biking over a hundred miles, I noticed there was a big, steep hill to get into Chattahoochee. I gritted my teeth as I huffed and puffed up the steep hill, and just in case I wasn't frustrated enough, it started to rain. I was sweating pretty well, so instead of stopping to put rain gear on, I delighted in the refreshing shower.

Within a mile, I somehow made it to my Warmshower host's house without looking at the Google map of my phone. When I looked at my phone before it started to rain, I tried to memorize the directions to my host's house. Amazingly I remembered well as I got to my host's home just before the heavens opened up.

My host was super friendly, but his dogs were barking up a storm. Once they smelled me and recognized I was not a threat, they quieted down. My host showed me into his home that was damaged by the hurricane six months earlier. My host shared many stories about living through bad hurricanes while living in Florida. He labeled his storm damaged home as "a work in progress." My host has been hosting cyclists for over fifteen years and was an adventure cyclist himself. It was ironic that his dream was to someday move to Bellingham, Washington, so he had lots of questions for me. It felt good to be out of the elements and in a warm home. After some conversation, my host went to work, but he left me in his house to stay for the evening. He showed me the shower, the kitchen where I was welcome to any food, and where I could sleep for the evening. The dogs were in their cage on the porch, so I had peace in the house. I was surprised my host was so trusting of me, but most people view cyclists as safe people because it is not like I am going to steal a large screen TV and carry it on my bike.

## Day 42 – (44 miles) Chattahoochee to Tallahassee, Florida

> *"Twenty years from now you will be more disappointed by the things you didn't do than by the ones you did do."*
> – Mark Twain

I woke up at my usual time, got my things together, and left before my host got home. I would have loved to talk to my host further, but I noticed more thunderstorms were forecast that day. I wanted to bike the 44 miles to Tallahassee before it started to rain. The roads were already very wet as I must have been just behind the storm cell because it never rained on me, although it always looked dark and scary just ahead of me.

In Tallahassee, I had two Warmshower hosts to choose from, as they both got back to me at the same time. One was a rather large operation that took in a lot of cyclists, and the other was a family. I decided to choose the family.

It had been a while since I had a dog chasing me, and I had my guard down and was no longer flinching after seeing any movement in my periphery. Unfortunately, I looked ahead and saw a dog that appeared to be pitbull mix waiting for me in his driveway. Since he was not barking, I decided to move to the other side of the road, as there was little traffic on the road at the time. I reached into my handlebar bag to grab my pepper spray. The pepper spray was my last resort because I did not want to injure the dog in any way. As I got closer to the dog, it started barking and was looking like he was preparing himself to chase me. Typically, on my bike trip to date, I would yell "Go Home" to dogs that were chasing me, but I had a realization that this did not work, and I needed a new strategy or saying. As I got closer to the dog, which looked intimidating and fast, I looked right into its eyes and yelled with my most authoritative voice, "STAY!!!" The dog looked confused as it wanted to run but was just told to stay. At first, it stayed but slowly started coming at me again. As I saw it starting to pick up speed, I yelled back, "STAY!!" The dog stopped, stayed, but I could tell it was having cognitive dissonance because its instinct was to chase. With the dog's hesitation, I began to pull well ahead of it, and the dog after my second "STAY!!" decided not to pursue me. I felt good that I got through that scary situation through words and not my pepper spray. It would be the last dog to give chase to me on my trip.

After some flat road riding and biking through the campus of Florida State University, I biked on the side streets to my host's home.

My hosts were a young couple who were adventure cyclists themselves. They participated in bike races of four hundred miles and were planning a trip to France to compete in a long bike race. They were super friendly, had a spare bed in their kid's playroom, and their place was very comfortable. A bonus is they made a super healthy meal that I desperately needed considering all the fast food I had been eating the past few days. I was surprised I hadn't had a heart attack with all the McDonalds I had eaten. Salad, a green drink, and lots of vegetables were a welcome sight even though I do not like eating vegetables.

I was excited for the next day as I would achieve my vision of biking to a friend's office on the campus of Valdosta State University. Initially, I wanted to surprise him, but (a) I had told him I was coming, and (b) he was following me on Facebook. My goal was to make it to his office at the university by 4 pm so I could attend a special ring ceremony for the players and coaches of the Division 2 National Football Champions.

### Day 43 – (85 miles) Tallahassee, Florida to Valdosta, Georgia

*"There is nothing on this earth more to be prized than true friendship."*
*– Thomas Aquinas*

A great lesson I learned on my travels was to talk to the locals for helpful shortcuts. The night before, my Warmshower host showed me an alternate route, as Valdosta was not on the ACA southern tier route. The shortcut would shorten my ride to Valdosta by 18 miles.

My Warmshower host had told me the terrain was going to be hilly as we were in the foothills of the Appalachian Mountains. I biked on rural roads outside Tallahassee before I got onto the busy Route 90. The riding was fantastic, and I seemed to be full of energy. I was biking with great focus and speed. My first destination was Monticello, Florida, where I would take a Gatorade break but then find a restaurant for a second full breakfast as it looked like Monticello would be the largest town I would bike through before I entered Valdosta.

After an excellent second breakfast of bacon and eggs at a local diner, I was off to take the shortcut my Warmshower host told me about and headed to Country Road 149, which was a good biking road with little traffic. The most crucial part of riding this road was at some point there was a right I needed to take to head toward Valdosta.

While it is great to be in flow and be so deep in thought of life or more likely the logistics of the ride that you're oblivious of time and place, it can be an issue when you miss your crucial right turn. I remember seeing a sign that said the road headed toward Boston, Georgia, and I was so enamored with the idea that there was a Boston in Georgia, and wondered what it was like there, that I forgot about the right turn that I needed to take to Valdosta. I did not know the name of the road because my map app was not detailed enough. Unfortunately for me, I did not think I missed my right turn until I was five miles past the turn and only three miles from Boston, which was about ten miles off course. At this point, I was so upset at myself that f-bombs were coming out of me in a staccato manner. It took a long time for me to gather myself as I was determined to correct my self-inflicted mistake by first getting to Boston, which I now loathed. My best bet was to continue cycling and use my negative energy to propel me forward towards Valdosta. In the big picture, I was making great time and was way ahead of schedule. If I had not missed my turn, I probably would have been rolling into Valdosta at just before noon.

I ended up in Valdosta by 1 pm. I texted my friend, and he told me to be on his campus by 1:30 pm, so I slowly made my way to the Valdosta State University (VSU) campus, where my friend is the president of the university. He surprised me with some of his cabinet cheering me on as I biked through a finish line tape. The plan was for me to arrive at around 4 pm, and there was an even bigger celebration planned, so I caught everyone off guard by showing up early. It was a nice touch, and it was good to see my friend Rich and his colleagues.

While I didn't surprise my friend Rich in his office like I initially visualized at the beginning of my trip; however, I still surprised him by just showing up on my bike after biking over three thousand miles to get to his office. If he thought I was a bit of a lunatic before I arrived, arriving at his office on my bike from California indeed confirmed it.

Since it was near graduation, it was quieter on campus. The ring ceremony was not until about 5 pm, so we had time to catch up in his office. It is funny because Rich always tells me he lives vicariously through my adventures (of which I have done many), but I say to Rich I live vicariously through his successful career, especially seeing that he is president of a thriving university. Rich is a president, and I am a semi-retired adventurer. Rich and I had gone to graduate school together at Southern Illinois University at Carbondale (SIUC) twenty-four years ago. We hung out together in and out of class and were mentored by the late Dr. James Wallace (JAW), who we both loved. We arrived at our graduate program during a tumultuous time, especially with the hiring of JAW as the new department chair. I would be JAW's first recruit to the program and ended up helping JAW, Rich, and the rest of the first-year graduate students get the program back on its feet. Whenever Rich and I get together, we loved to revisit stories of the beloved chair of our department and the wonderful times we had during graduate school at SIUC.

After some reminiscing and catching up, I got cleaned up and went to the ring ceremony. Many people at Valdosta State University asked me about my bike trip, and I was always welcome to share my story. Surprisingly, I was feeling very relaxed and energetic for having ridden 85 miles, but it could have been the adrenalin rush of seeing Rich and for having only one more day to complete a dream.

At the ring ceremony, Rich, as President of Valdosta State University, passed out rings to the coaches and players of the University's

Division 2 National Football Champions. I was pleased to have attended such a special event. I chuckled at how some of the players made Rich look so small.

After the event, we went back to his house, and I was happy to reconnect with his wife, also an SIUC alum, and his two growing teenagers. It was great to see everyone, and I was much appreciative of their generosity and hospitality during my stay.

### Day 44 – Zero-Day, Valdosta, Georgia

> *"Take a rest; a field that has rested gives a bountiful crop."*
> *– Ovid*

I decided to take a zero-day, and the second cup of coffee did not initiate it. It was only my second zero-day of my trip. A zero-day was what it sounded like, bike zero miles, and stay off the bike to rest and rejuvenate my weary muscles. I took the day to eat a substantial amount of food, including lots of steak and chicken. I also lounged around Rich's comfortable house and took everything slowly. I purposely was sloth-like all day. It was a chance to do laundry, start the process of getting my gear ready to be shipped home, and recharge my energy plant as the last day of riding would be a doozy.

I also received a text from Ed that he finished his ride across America in St. Augustine, Florida. I had met Ed at the Desert Inn in Brawley, California, and we biked together for a couple of significant portions of the ride, most notably the 120-mile windy ride from Lordsburg to Las Cruces in New Mexico. We remained in contact by text throughout the trip and did bump into each last in East Texas. I was happy for Ed finishing. After congratulating each other for finishing a challenging ride, we agreed to meet up in about a week when I flew into Boston's Logan Airport to see family.

## THE SOUTHERN TIER BICYCLE ROUTE RIDE ENDS

### Day 45 – (132 miles) Valdosta, Georgia to Amelia Island, Florida

*"So many of our dreams at first seem impossible, then seem improbable, and then when we summon the will, will soon seem inevitable."*

– Christopher Reeve

The last day, Rich and I woke up very early to head to – where else? – the local McDonalds for a big breakfast and a medium coffee. Usually, I rarely go to McDonalds in my regular life, but when I am on an adventure trip and am in a pressing need for a heavy meal that hits the spot, McDonalds never disappoints.

After breakfast, Rich and I drove over to the parking lot in front of his office on the VSU campus. I loaded up my bike and gave Rich an estimation of when I believed I would be at our agreed-upon rendezvous point, which was a Dunkin Donuts outside of Amelia Island. I was feeling terrific as I had not been on my bike for a day and a half and had been eating quite a bit of food in the last thirty-six hours. So, I was energized to take on the challenge of biking a hundred and twenty five miles. I was a little concerned that I was not on a bike route, but the route I mapped out was the only logical way to get to Amelia Island from Valdosta. The road had me biking through the Okefenokee Swamp area, with over ten thousand alligators that call it home.

The light was still dim as I began, and the traffic was light at 6:20 am. Just outside of Valdosta, I would get on highway 94 for about twenty miles to the town of Statenville, Georgia. It was a tiny town, and it only had one convenience store. I knew I was going to need to take a break here as the next town of Fargo, Georgia, was another thirty miles away. As I saw the town store, I heard a lot of commotion and noticed a group of locals sitting around a table having a discussion. Not knowing the individuals, I felt vulnerable and self-conscious walking by in my tight spandex bike shorts, knowing they probably did not see a lot of bike tourists bike through their town. I locked up my bike on the other side of the store of the men at the table, but as I was trying to walk discreetly into the store to buy a Gatorade, the men at the table asked me what I was doing? And then invited me to "the table of wisdom." Just as one of the gentlemen labeled themselves, "the table of wisdom," another local walked by and called out "more like the table of bullshit." There was lots of laughter after the comment, including from myself. I felt a little more comfortable with the table of wisdom and told them I was biking across America and that I needed to use the restroom and buy a Gatorade. I then said to them I'd stop by their table on my return.

After taking care of business, I stopped by the table of wisdom. The gentleman, some of them retired, were locals of Statenville, who mostly worked in the lumber industry. They confirmed that they did not see many bike tourists but were intrigued, and asked me all sorts of questions that clued me in that they were clueless about bike touring. I was happy to answer all of their questions. The Georgia gents were hilarious and whimsical and were working on laughs at my expense. But I was able to keep up and dish where appropriate. At one point, one of them asked how I could ride my bike on the road with all the logging trucks flying by me? They asked, "How do you do it? Aren't you afraid?" I responded by turning sideways and thumbing toward my back, saying, "you need one of these." They didn't understand. I then said slowly, clearly, and with emphasis, "you need a backbone to bike across America." The table thought this was the funniest thing they ever heard. We got along excellently, and the table I was concerned about at first was now a rousing good time, but I knew I could not stay long because I still had more than a hundred miles to go. The gents at the table wished me luck, and I wished them well before I was off towards Fargo, Georgia.

Highway 94 was straight, flat, there was little wind in the morning, and I was always on the lookout for alligators since I was near the Okefenokee Swamp. Periodically, logging trucks would drive by, but they gave me lots of space. Traffic was very light on Highway 94, and by 10 am, I had made it to Fargo, the fifty-mile mark, for what turned out to be my second breakfast at a buffet in the local diner. I ate as much as I could and drank as much coffee as they would allow. After fueling myself up, I headed toward Florida.

After leaving Fargo, to entertain myself, I got an earworm of a song I saw on a friend's Facebook feed. The post my friend made was innocent enough. It was labeled the top twenty songs of 1971. One of the songs on the list was "Do You Know What I Mean?" by Lee Michaels. I loved that song and hadn't thought about it in years. A few nights before, I found the song on YouTube and played it repeatedly. Now that I was on a hundred and twenty-five mile bike ride and on a straight road with no traffic with a mind looking for activity, I began singing Lee Michael's song to myself, and then to whoever wanted to hear it for the next four hours. It was fun, and it indeed preoccupied my mind for many miles. It also distracted me as for the last seventy-five miles there was an annoying twelve mph steady headwind. I asked the heavens why, on my last day, there had to be a headwind to make a challenging bike ride even more challenging? However, it wasn't worth getting too worked up over, so I just gutted it out and kept singing to myself.

I was at the 100-mile mark when I saw, on the side of the road, my friend Rich holding a Gatorade in his hand. It was great to see him and have a quick little break. I didn't tell him but I was going to stop at the McDonalds that was just down the street because I had not eaten anything in hours, but since I knew he would be waiting for me at Dunkin Donuts that was about fifteen miles away I felt compelled to skip the McDonalds and gut it out all the way to our rendezvous point. The headwind seemed to be getting worse, or it could have been I was getting weaker. As I got closer to being on the outskirts of Amelia Island, the road construction was downright dangerous as there were no bike lanes on Highway 200, and I had to ride close to the speeding cars and trucks on the highway which increased the "pucker factor." I was so close to finishing. I started to think about how much it would suck if I got hit, or worse, killed by a car or truck on this highway, especially since I was so close to finishing. With the danger factor so high, it was not out of the realm of the impossible. A few people honked their horns at me, but there was nowhere I could go, and I did not see a better alternative.

I finally met Rich at the Dunkin Donut meeting spot. I had biked well over a hundred miles and had not eaten since 10 am in Fargo. Rich was ready to go, but I told him I needed to lie on the grass a minute. I had thought about getting a couple of donuts and an iced coffee, but I hated to have Rich wait as I appreciated the fact that he wanted to ride the last part with me. Also, I thought if I sat too long in the Dunkin Donuts, I might seize up and may never want to start again, especially after the lactic acid invaded my body. Rich was willing to wait, but I also wanted to finish. It would be a big moment for me, and I had the opportunity to share it with a great friend. Rich was excited to get started, and I warned him about the road construction. Rich would follow me as I had the map app. After a couple of miles in the road construction, we were back in the breakdown lane, and it was smooth sailing to Amelia Island beach.

As we got closer, it seemed unreal that I was about to accomplish a dream. My excitement seemed muted as I just biked a hundred and twenty five miles. I was hungry, dehydrated, and I wasn't thinking too clearly. As we got to the beachfront, I took off my bike shoes and put on Teva's so the sand would not wreak sandy havoc on my bike shoes. As we got closer to the ocean, it seemed Rich was more excited than I was at the accomplishment as he started telling people around us that I just biked across America. Typically, people biking the southern tier finish in St. Augustine. The people of St. Augustine are used to cross country cyclists, but at Amelia Island, it was different. People started wanting their picture with me as if I was a celebrity. It was fun getting the recognition, and it was fun seeing how excited Rich and the others were with the accomplishment.

Once I got the panorama of the beach, and the beautiful Atlantic Ocean, the biggest, most genuine smile of my life grew on my face as I knew I had accomplished a seemingly impossible goal. While outwardly, I was exhausted; however, inwardly, I felt the same way I feel listening to the rousing final chorus of "More Than a Feeling" by the rock group Boston. A chorus that makes you feel powerful, invincible, and overjoyed at the same time. I knew I was experiencing a magical moment to cherish. Seeing the ocean made me feel like anything in life is possible. I finally did it and it was a great feeling.

The last thing I needed to do and to document my accomplishment was to place my front wheel in the Atlantic Ocean, signifying the end of the cross-country ride. I picked up my bike to carry it over the soft sand. I did not bike with all my gear on the last day and only had the essentials on the back of my bike because I knew Rich was going to be with me and drive me back to Valdosta.

Once I plunked the front wheel into the ocean, it was over. Rich took some pictures, and others took photos of Rich and me. It was an exciting moment that warranted hugs and high fives. Others walking by congratulated me on my accomplishment. Some had questions. One woman with a group of six young kids came over to have the kids ask questions. Just before they came over, Rich popped out a celebratory beer, and we toasted to the accomplishment. The funny thing is the alcohol in the beer seemed to mess with my dehydrated body, and I was getting woozy. As if I was instantly drunk and my blood pressure tanked. I was light-headed, but I was also pumping a lot of adrenalin because I was so excited about finishing. The woman with the kids asked me what I ate throughout the trip. She assumed I ate healthy food. Rich began laughing because he knew the truth. I didn't want to bust the friendly woman's bubble, but I didn't want to lie, so I gave my standard line that "my body was fueled

# THE SOUTHERN TIER BICYCLE ROUTE RIDE ENDS

by McDonalds." She looked aghast and didn't seem to believe it, and then she turned indignant by stating I should have eaten healthier because then I would have been stronger. I did not want to have a debate, so I partially agreed with her and left it at that. I then turned my attention to answering questions and taking pictures with the kids. At first, I still had my beer can in my hand but realized the optics of the photograph were awkward, so I gave Rich the beer can to hold.

Once all the people left Rich and me alone, I reflected a minute on what an accomplishment it was and how fortunate I was to share it with Rich. My original vision was to bike across America and surprise Rich in his office. I never thought he would take time out of his busy day as president of a large university to bike with me and celebrate with me on Amelia Island. I also reflected on when I was at the Pacific Ocean, thinking how the hell am I going to make it to the Atlantic Ocean, and now that I was at the Atlantic Ocean, I couldn't believe I made it and wondered how the hell did that happen. It was a great feeling that would take days for me to process.

We eventually left the beach, and Rich treated me to dinner at the restaurant where we entered the beach with our bikes. The food was great, and it seriously energized me. The ride back to the car was surprisingly easy as I thought the stoppage of riding would cause harmful lactic acid build-up, but it did not. I felt great once we got to the car and could have kept going back to Valdosta. However, we loaded the bikes into Rich's SUV and drove back to Valdosta. The irony of driving back was that even though it was very comfortable and only took a little over two hours to drive the hundred and twenty or so miles to Valdosta, it seemed to take forever, and I kept falling asleep. It seemed when I was on my bike, time was not a factor, and it was more fun. I never even thought of the miles because I was super focused, engaged, and in flow, as well as preoccupied singing Lee Michaels song "Do You Know What I Mean?"

## Chapter 10: Bike Trip Stats

*"If you place the coins of your purse into your mind, your mind will fill your pockets with gold."*
– Benjamin Franklin

Trip stats:
- 3,411 miles biked in 43 biking days (79 miles per day)
- 45-day trip (only two zero-days - Phoenix, Arizona and Valdosta, Georgia) - 7 days on the west coast plus 38 days on the southern tier bicycle route.
- Started in Salinas, California then biked to San Diego and then to Amelia Island, Florida
- Zero flats (only one slow leak for 876 miles from Van Horn, Texas that I finally fixed in my motel room in Kountze, Texas)
- Bike repairs: bottom bracket, chain, rear cartridge replaced, front and back brakes serviced, damaged bike post repaired, and gear issues resolved for a cost of $243 and only slightly over two hours of downtime – bike mechanics were awesome and made my repairs their priority
- 20,640 minutes (or 344 hours) riding my bike – no wonder saddle sores were a big concern
- One duct taped shoe that lasted all 3,411 miles of biking
- Chased by 27 dogs in 3 states – Texas, Louisiana, and Florida
- Wind: 50% headwinds; 25% crosswinds; 15% tailwinds; 10% no wind
- No rainy days: Only 2 hours of light rain, and 2 foggy, misty mornings
- Coldest morning: 27 degrees in Marfa, Texas
- Hottest day: 92 degrees in Del Rio, Texas
- No injuries during the trip (unless you count the saddle sores)
- Never once wanted to quit as I was too motivated to finish
- Places to sleep:
  — 15 Warmshower hosts
  — 11 nights camping
  — 8 nights with friends
  — 11 nights in a cheap motel
- Ate at McDonalds 50 times (1.2x per riding day – consistent, high fat, comfortable, and inexpensive). Also, I ate at other fast food

venues another 15 times – not proud of myself, but it seemed necessary.
- Lost 18 pounds
- Experiencing a dream trip, providing beautiful memories, and accomplishing a seemingly impossible goal: priceless

## Chapter 11: Cost Breakdown of Bike Trip

*"Experience, whether good or bad, can't be bought with the finest gold because the journey in itself is priceless."*
— Anonymous

Food/Snacks: $1,200 (McDonalds = $400+: 33+% of total)
Motels/KOA: $667 (11 nights)
Bike/camping gear: $273
Bike repairs: $243
Camping: $117 (11 nights)
Laundry: $11 (2x)
CVS (Drug Store): $39 (for saddle sores)
Transportation: $362 (Amtrak/ flights home)
Ship bike/gear: $286
*Total Cost:*$3,200 (or $71/day or $57/biking day)

It cost money to bike across America, and while I tried to keep my expenses under control, it was hard to do so especially toward the end of the trip. I thought I did a pretty good job. However, other touring cyclists spend on average as little as $10 per biking day, and I also heard $29 per biking day, but I am satisfied with my $57 per biking day. It is hard for me to comprehend how I spent $1,200 on food, but I realized that the more miles I rode, the more I needed to eat at least four meals a day. Whatever budget I thought I was on was shot because I splurged on snacks, food, and Gatorade because my body needed it. I did cook some meals to help save money. I usually spend about $300 a month for food when I am at home, but when biking eighty miles per day, I needed some serious calories to stop me from bonking. Even more amazing was that many of my Warmshower hosts and friends either made or bought me breakfast, lunch, or dinner, and I still spent $1200 on food.

It is also interesting to note during half my nights, Warmshower hosts or friends hosted me. So, my housing cost could have been a lot higher. Bike repairs and purchasing of gear were necessities. All three-bike mechanics at Jax Bicycle Center in San Clemente, the REI in Austin, and in Truly Spokin' in Milton, Florida, were the true heroes of my trip. They dropped everything, fixed my bike immediately, and I only lost two hours of downtime total. The two big gear purchases were a new $100 inflatable Thermarest sleeping mat (because I accidentally put a fork through my old one). The other, a new $60 pair of bike shorts to help my saddle sores situation. I did no wild camping like I wanted to try but did camp in a town park and the yard of a church. Cheap motels were necessary when the weather was stormy at night, I was having a challenging day, or when there were no safe alternatives.

## Chapter 12: Lessons Learned

*"Life is a long journey, with problems to solve, lessons to learn, but most of all, experiences to enjoy."*
– Anonymous

When I started my journey, I worried about everything about the trip. I was fully confident I could finish biking down the Pacific Coast. However, biking across the United States was where the real challenge and fear would present itself. I had no experience biking across deserts nor in especially remote areas like West Texas. There was no welcomed constant companion of a Pacific Ocean to revel at its beauty and get inspired. Resources were scarce in many places, and I had little experience being so alone on a bike in the middle of nowhere. I had all these irrational fears of meeting evil characters. They included dangerous biker gangs, ruthless drug traffickers, or deranged serial killers out in the middle of the desert where I was vulnerable. I feared getting lost and not having enough water. I also had worried I would get caught in a nasty thunderstorm or maybe even be found in a tornado. Possible dangers seemed to lurk everywhere on the ride. Before I began the trip, my fearmongering imagination was on maximum overdrive, and some of my friends and family did not help by bringing up "possibilities." Fear ran rampant, but I learned to listen to my concerns but not be ruled by them.

Biking across America was a tremendous growth experience for me in that I overcame all my fears and found most, if not all, were unfounded. I never met any nefarious characters. I only met exceptional people who were open, curious, and generous. It seemed to me I had some untold status or power that made me immune to evil and adverse events and encounters. I was more a magnet for fascination, awe, and goodwill. I think it was assumed by many I met that I was a nut chasing a dream. Many admired the "chutzpah" it takes to bike across America. Most wanted to do their part in helping me achieve my goal that somehow satisfied the dreamer in them. It never mattered who I came into contact with, whether a tattooed Harley biker, gangbanger, Apache Indian, trucker, rodeo enthusiast, Warmshower host, old, young, black, white, as everyone seemed to have questions about the ride, were good-natured, and the general response, whether verbalized or not, was that the endeavor was "bad-ass" and the person wished they could join me. It seemed like my ride appealed to something primitive within most people, and I believe it was the "adventurous spirit" that resides in all of us.

While there were many lessons learned on the trip, I highlight four:

**1 – A Model for Living**: It probably seems odd that I think biking across America is a model for living but hear me out. Most people I know, and I include myself in this statement, have worked jobs that no longer challenge or inspire us. We would wake up every day dreading going into the office. We spend eight or more hours toiling away and then scampering out to get a few hours rest before we get the opportunity to do it all over again the next day. Inevitable we can't wait for Friday and eventually, if we are lucky, to retire at 62 or 65. We think when we retire that we can live and do the things we always wanted to do but didn't have the time. It seemed to me like torture when participating in the rat race, but it was so typical. I've always thought there must be a better way to live.

While biking across America, I had an epiphany. There certainly is a different way to live daily life. I knew biking across America was a tremendous challenge and that I was privileged to have the opportunity to pursue my dream. I started with many fears; however, it was the personal challenge and goal that got me laser-focused to do my best. It was a model of living by being so focused and with a mission that inspired me. I woke up every morning, excited to get started. I had a simple routine to get ready, and I knew the next sixteen hours were a mystery. I didn't know what I would see, people I would meet, adversity I would encounter, but I looked forward to it all. I knew whatever kind of day I was going to have that it ultimately moved me toward my eventual goal of reaching the Atlantic Ocean. I was focused and lived simply. I felt comradeship with fellow bikers as well as warmth and compassion from strangers who were fascinated with my trip. I was working hard – exerting, sweating, and perhaps, cursing, but I was having fun. I had a purpose, I was free, and I felt alive. I felt the sun on my skin, smelled the fresh air, heard the waves crashing on the beach, and saw incredible beauty throughout my ride. There was no office drudgery, no useless meetings, and no office politics to tolerate. Just me on my bike, striving toward achieving a challenging goal, and doing what I needed to do to make it happen. It all made sense, and it felt good giving it my all. After a tough day of riding, I was exhausted. I had the satisfaction of feeling I accomplished something significant and thoroughly looked forward to doing it again the next day. To me, this was truly living. It was simple, challenging, mysterious, and free.

If only I could bottle the sense of being excited, alive, and free, I would be a truly wealthy man. It reminded me of the quote of Henry David Thoreau, who said, "the mass of men leads lives of quiet desperation." He wasn't talking about the men (or women) crossing the country on a bicycle.

**2 – When you want to achieve an impossible goal, do so by attaining many little goals:** The idea of biking across America seemed like an impossible task. Biking 3,411 miles also appears out of the realm of doable. I realized if I concentrated on the impossible task, then I would have never made it across America.

A better strategy was to keep my vision of reaching the Atlantic Ocean in my mind but tackling the seemingly impossible task with smaller, more doable goals. It is crucial when biking across the country to take one day at a time as if you were in a vacuum. You could easily get overwhelmed by the idea of crossing the country, but biking sixty to eighty miles in a day, especially if you started at the break of dawn, sounded more doable. You then can break the goals into even smaller chunks by challenging yourself to make it to the next town or the next McDonalds. My usual strategy was to try to bike twenty or thirty miles by the time I hit a city that might serve breakfast or had a convenience store. By having the carrot of food or rest just a town away, this small goal with a reward would propel me forward throughout the day.

Even during a challenging 38-mph headwind, I kept my attitude positive by challenging myself to make it to the next driveway, mailbox, or road sign. I knew I was in a bad situation that I had no control over. I would play mental gymnastics and challenge myself to reach small goals. It continuously propelled me forward. I would eventually be in a flow, and the compound effect took over to help me reach my final destination.

**3 – When pursuing an impossible goal, adversity is inevitable:** If you are going to attempt to achieve a bold, audacious goal, adversity will be inevitable so make adversity your friend. Difficulty such as strong headwinds, lousy weather, unleashed dogs, steep hills, bike trouble, saddle-sores, getting lost, almost getting hit by a truck, heat, finding a place to sleep, and many others will be a daily reality when biking across America.

While we all would love a stress-free ride across the country, it will not happen. So, it is best to recognize that adversity is inevitable and to prepare for its eventuality in advance. The most effective approach would be to be proactive when you can and to try to anticipate some of the adversity you might deal with within the next day or week. For example, I left at the end of March because I knew if I went earlier, it would be colder and the daylight would be shorter. However, if I left later, then I would be biking in much hotter temperatures in the desert and stormier weather in the southern states. By going when I did, I was proactive in creating a ride with delightful weather, little rain, and no storms. Proactive behavior helped deal with the wind by starting to bike early in the morning before the winds began. Checking directions before heading out to reduce getting lost and talking to locals about shortcuts that prevented encounters with dogs, provided safer roads, and better scenery was also an excellent proactive practice.

The second-best approach to adversity was to take a solution-focused approach. We are all human, so getting frustrated at an adverse situation is natural. However, all that frustration would create negative energy that would drain you of power you needed to accomplish your mission for the day. So, in situations where I got very frustrated, I would give myself five minutes to vent, then I would become solution-focused. If I were having a hard time calming down, I would take a long Gatorade break and not start until I regrouped. I found it essential to live in the moment thinking about what you can do in the present and not thinking about what happened in the past or what could happen in the future. You can't control the past or the future; you can only control the now.

Another benefit of promoting a positive attitude during my ride is that I noticed I would be luckier in attracting more goodwill or beneficial events. It was a manifestation of the "law of attraction." It worked. I think this was my superpower in attracting positive, friendly people who boosted my spirits and made my day.

It was also essential to concentrate on self-care while riding. I took it upon myself to take a lot of water breaks, eat well (relatively speaking), and reduce my mileage if my body needed rest.

While adversity was inevitable, how you prepared yourself and how you responded to the adversity could make or break your tour and affect how much you enjoy the ride.

**4 –People are important:** Throughout my life, I have been a bit of a loner and prided myself for being self-reliant, so the idea of biking across America solo and self-supported appealed to me. However, while I enjoyed being solo, I also loved the company. In 2017, I enjoyed biking half my days down the Oregon/California coast with Eduardo from Barcelona, Spain. We biked at our own pace but met up for breakfast, coffee, dinner, and camping. My expectation for biking across the country was to start solo but join up with a fellow biker. However, this was not to be. I met only two bikers who I biked a couple of days each with, and enjoyed, but never partnered with them in working together to complete the whole journey.

A profound discovery on my ride was the fact that even though I biked 3,411 miles predominantly solo, I never felt alone. I realized I shared the journey with many others and that people are essential. The people I met at convenience stores and McDonalds, fellow bikers, Warmshower hosts, motel owners, waitresses, locals, longtime friends, friend's moms, my girlfriend Ann, my Toastmasters friends, and many others were a big part of my trip. I was immensely grateful for all the love, support, hospitality, generosity, and warmth shown by everyone.

Again, while I was biking solo, I never felt alone, and that made a massive difference in helping me achieve the dream of biking across America. Many times, reading from other adventurer's blogs, they would write how they were overwhelmed by the outpouring of generosity they experienced on their journey. It gave them a newfound appreciation for people in general. I now have first-hand experience with what they were talking about as I experienced it many times on my trip.

Biking across America was indeed a journey of discovery, and the lessons learned will benefit me for the better for the rest of my life.

## Chapter 13: Last Reflections

> *"It is not the critic who counts; not the man who points out how the strong man stumbles, or where the doer of deeds could have done them better. The credit belongs to the man who is actually in the arena, whose face is marred by dust and sweat and blood; who strives valiantly; who errs, who comes short again and again, because there is no effort without error and shortcoming; but who does actually strive to do the deeds; who knows great enthusiasms, the great devotions; who spends himself in a worthy cause; who at the best knows in the end the triumph of high achievement, and who at the worst, if he fails, at least fails while daring greatly, so that his place shall never be with those cold and timid souls who neither know victory nor defeat."*
> – Theodore Roosevelt

Wow! It is over. I can't understand why it seems unreal that I accomplished the feat of biking across the United States. The other day I woke up from a deep sleep thinking about the idea of biking across America and then realized I had already completed it. Holy cow! I can't believe it. My mind and body still haven't processed the accomplishment. I vividly remember hearing the waves crash onto the beautiful sandy beach of the Atlantic Ocean and then dipping my front wheel into the ocean, signifying the achievement of a dream. Yet, part of my psyche still hadn't grasped that the accomplishment was real.

It amazed me to think of all the fears I had before I started my journey. They almost stopped me from starting; however, by pushing through and having the intestinal fortitude to take on the challenge, I accomplished a dream and became a stronger person. It solidified the thought that nothing is impossible if you put your mind, effort, and resources towards your goal in a very focused manner.

As a result of biking across America, my perceptions of America have changed. For example:

**I will never look at a map of the United States the same way.** I use to look at a map and dream about biking across America. Now I look at a map, and the vision is a reality. Biking across America looked impossible six months ago, but now I know it is possible. A map of the USA is a reminder of my history, a good time, and a tremendous accomplishment. I like to follow my route down the west coast and across America and remember all the people I met and the good times I had on my journey.

**Places I visited will have new meaning and memories.** Looking at the Big Sur on the map has a new meaning as I remember biking down it in awe of the natural beauty and the wonderment of camping under the redwood trees. Crossing the Imperial Valley brings memories of strong winds, friendly people, and wide-open spaces. The state of Louisiana means the greenest country, the most exceptional hosts, and the warmest people. And finally, the Atlantic Ocean was a large body of water, but now means the accomplishment of a dream.

**American cultures will be better understood.** After experiencing thirteen days in Texas, I have a better understanding of Texas pride. Southern charm and hospitality have new personal meaning, and Phoenix retirement communities were a great experience that I might want to try again in the future.

**Common words will have new meaning.** When someone says "hospitality," I now think of all the Warmshower hosts, friends, and friends of friends who were impressive in their hospitality while hosting me. "People power" means the power of people, friends, and strangers who inspired me, help me overcome tough times, and help me move toward my dreams. The word "friendliness" conjures up all the strangers I met along my ride that asked me questions, shared their experiences, laughed and joked, and made my day.

The accomplishment is real, and the memories will last a lifetime. I hope people reading this book will get the idea that biking across America is possible for everyone. If you take the challenge, you will discover the beauty of the people and the land called the United States of America. By taking that challenge, you will grow as a person and create new meanings that will shape your world for the better and stretch what you believed was possible. In the end, you will realize you were not just biking across America; you were learning what a great country we live in.

# Epilogue

*"A great accomplishment shouldn't be the end of the road, just the starting point for the next leap forward."*
*– Harvey Mackay*

I get asked all the time – What is next? When asked, especially during question and answer sessions after a presentation about my bike trip across America, I get stumped. I can't think of anything I am interested in doing that would be as big an undertaking as biking across America. I could bike the Northern Tier or hike the Pacific Crest Trail, but I have no real desire to do it. I've thought about walking the Camino De Santiago or hiking the Tour Du Mont Blanc in Europe, but both are too crowded.

My next project was trying to write this book and hopefully inspire others to pursue their dreams. I have to admit writing this book was a lot harder and time-consuming than biking across America. I seemed to have instincts and the ability to bike but struggled to put to words what I experienced. As the saying goes, "what doesn't kill you makes you stronger". The writing of the book was hard, but as the ride across America, what is hard is also most rewarding.

As for future adventure trips, over the last fifteen years, I have biked and hiked all over the western United States, including hiking the John Muir Trail, the beautiful Wind River Range, all over the North Cascades and the Canadian Rockies. If I had an ultimate adventure to pursue next, it would be hiking in the wild Kluane National Park in the Yukon and the Wrangell-St. Elias National Park in Alaska. Both parks are wild, remote, and scare the shit out of me. That might be why I want to go. Perhaps, it is time to call my mom and see what she thinks of my new idea.

## Author Bio

Patrick McGinty is a semi-retired, lifelong adventure seeker and author of the travel memoir "A Bike Ride Across America: A 3,411 Mile Journey of Discovery".  Patrick writes it likes he experienced it in his honest, amusing, and introspective look at achieving the dream of biking across America self-supported.  Patrick has a M.A. Speech Communications from Emerson College, a M.S. Higher Education Administration from Southern Illinois University at Carbondale, and an MBA Finance from Johnson & Wales University. He is a former member of the United States Marine Corps, a Distinguished Toastmaster (DTM), and disciple of Mr. Money Mustache ("a mustachian"). Patrick lives in Bellingham, Washington and loves to hike and bike throughout the Pacific Northwest, the Canadian Rockies (his favorite), and the Wind River Range in Wyoming.

# Colophon

This book was edited and designed by Jeffrey Copeland at Bywater Press, Bellingham, Washington during the winter of 2020. The text is set in Hiroshige Book with Lucida Sans as the display type. The book was set using the TeX typesetting system and custom-developed software for automatically converting files from Microsoft Word to TeX, along with other open source software tools.

Hiroshige was designed by Cynthia Hollandsworth Batty and released by AlphaOmega in 1986. It is named after nineteenth-century Japanese artist and printmaker Utagawa Hiroshige, who travelled the Tōkaidō road from Edo to Kyoto in 1832, painting *The Fifty-three Stations of the Tōkaidō* from his journey.

The Lucida font family was designed by Charles Bigelow and Kris Holmes beginning in 1984. The version used here was released by Adobe Systems in 1987.

TeX was developed by mathematician and computer scientist Donald Knuth. It was originally released in 1978 and intended for printing mathematical textbooks, however, it is equally suited for high-quality, general-purpose typesetting.

The photographs in this volume and on its cover were provided by the author. The Mercator projection route maps were created for Bywater Press by Lawrence Gill based on data obtained from the Massachusetts Institute of Technology.

www.bywaterpress.com

www.ingramcontent.com/pod-product-compliance
Lightning Source LLC
Chambersburg PA
CBHW071450080526
44587CB00014B/2057